The Ponytail Girls

Meet The Ponytail Girls

Other books in
The Ponytail Girls series:

Book 2
The Impossible Christmas Present

Book 3
Lost on Monster Mountain

Book 4
A Stormy Spring

Book 5
Escape from Camp Porcupine

Book 6
What's Up With Her?

The Ponytail Girls

Meet The Ponytail Girls

Bonnie Compton Hanson

Dedication

To each girl who reads this book and becomes a PT,
filling with joy your own life
and the lives of all you meet.

THE PONYTAIL GIRLS/BOOK 1: MEET THE PONYTAIL GIRLS

ISBN 10: 1-58411-029-5
ISBN 13: 978-1-58411-029-3
Legacy reorder# LP48041

Legacy Press
P.O. Box 261129
San Diego, CA 92196

Illustrator: Aline Heiser

Printed in the United States of America

Contents

~ Introduction ~

Welcome to the Ponytail Girls! Whether you wear a ponytail or not you can share in the adventures of Sam Pearson and her friends, the PTs (that's short for Ponytails!). Just like you, the PTs love sports and shopping and fun with their friends at school.

The PTs also want to live in a way that is pleasing to God. So when they have problems and conflicts, they look to God and His Word, the Bible. They might also seek help from their parents, their pastor or their Sunday school class teacher, just like you do.

Each chapter in this book presents a new problem for your PTs to solve. Then there is a Bible story to help explain the Christian value that the PTs learned. A Bible memory verse is included for you to practice and share.

There may be words in this book that are new to you, especially some Bible names and Spanish words. Look them up in the Glossary on page 199, then use the syllables to sound out the words.

In addition to the stories, in each chapter you will find questions to answer and fun quizzes, puzzles and other activities. Also, at the end of each chapter starting with Chapter 3, you get a Secret Letter clue for the Secret Birthday Circle. See if you can guess what it says before all the clues are in!

The fun doesn't end with the stories. At the end of the book, there are pages for you to list your Prayer Partners and Prayer Requests. There's even a Sweet Dreams Diary section. You might want to copy these pages so that you have more space for writing. You'll also find information and membership cards in the back of the book for starting your own Ponytail Girls Club.

This first Ponytail Girls book begins just before school starts in the fall. The next four books continue on through the school year and into the following summer. So as soon as you finish this book, Sam and her friends want to share more PTs adventures with you. Now, let's meet the PTs!

Meet the Ponytail Girls!

• Who Are They? •

The PTs are girls your age who enjoy school, church, shopping and being with their friends and family. They also love meeting new friends. Friends just like you! You will like being a part of their lives.

The Ponytail Girls all attend Madison Middle School in the small town of Circleville. They're all also members of Miss Kotter's Sunday school class at nearby Faith Church on Sunday mornings. On Sunday evenings, they attend the special Zone 56 group for guys and girls in fifth and sixth grade. Their pastor is Rev. J. T. McConahan, and their youth leader is Pastor Andrew Garretti, whom they call "Pastor Andy."

Sam and Sara grew up in Circleville. Le's and LaToya's families moved into their neighborhood last year. When Sam and Sara met them at school, they invited them to church. Now it would be difficult for them to imagine not being Ponytail Girls! And as each new member joins, she feels the same way.

How did the PTs get their club name? Well, as you can see from their pictures, they all wear a ponytail of one kind or another. So that's what their other friends and families started calling them just for fun. Then one day LaToya shortened it to "PTs." Now that's what they all call themselves!

The PTs' club meetings are held whenever they can all get together. The girls have a secret motto: PT4JC, which means "Ponytails for Jesus Christ." But most of the time they don't want to keep secrets. They want to share with everyone the Good News about their best friend, Jesus.

So have fun sharing in your PTs' adventures. Laugh with them in their silly times, think and pray with them through their problems. And learn with them that the answers to all problems can be found right in God's Word. Keep your Bible and a sharpened pencil handy. Sam and the others are waiting for you!

Get To Know The PTs

Sam Pearson *has a long blond ponytail, sparkling blue eyes and a dream: she wants to play professional basketball. She also likes to design clothes. Sam's real name is "Samantha," but her friends and family just call her "Sam" for short. Sam's little brother, Petie, is 6. Joe, her dad, is great at fixing things, like cars and bikes. Her mom, Jean, bakes scrumptious cakes and pies and works at the Paws and Pooches Animal Shelter. Sneezit is the family dog.*

• Sam Pearson •

LaToya Thomas' *black curls are ponytailed high above her ears. That way she doesn't miss a thing going on! LaToya's into gymnastics and playing the guitar. Her big sister, Tina, is in college, training to be a nurse. Her mom is a school teacher; her dad works nights at a supermarket. Also living with the Thomases is LaToya's beloved, wheelchair-bound grandmother, Granny B.*

• LaToya Thomas •

Le Tran *parts her glossy black hair to one side, holding it back with one small ponytail. She loves sewing, soccer and playing the violin. Her mother, Viola, a concert pianist, often plays duets with her. Her father, Daniel, died in an accident. Mrs. Tran is a Buddhist from Vietnam, but Mr. Tran became a Christian before he died. Le is praying that her mother will become one, too.*

Sara Fields *lives down the street from Sam. She keeps her fiery, red hair from flying away by tying it into a ponytail flat against each side of her head. Sara has freckles, glasses and a great sense of humor. She loves to sing. She also loves softball, ice skating and cheerleading. Sara has a big brother, Tony, and a big dog, Tank. Both her parents are artists.*

When **Maria Moreno** *moves in next door to Sam in Chapter 3, she becomes the fifth PT. Maria pulls part of her long, brown hair into one topknot ponytail at the back; the rest hangs loose. She is tall, the way basketball-lover Sam would like to be! But Maria's into science, not basketball. At home, she helps her mother take care of her 6-year-old twin brothers, Juan and Ricardo, and a little sister, Lolita. The Morenos all speak Spanish as well as English.*

Miss Kitty Kotter, *the girls' Sunday school teacher, is not a PT, but she is an important part of their lives both in and out of church. Miss Kotter works as a computer engineer. She also loves to go on hikes. Her boyfriend, Bob Ingram, is in the Navy, so he is out to sea most of the time. Miss Kotter calls the Bible her "how-to book" because, she says, it tells "how to" live. Miss Kotter volunteers at the Circleville Rescue Mission.*

Chapter 1

Help, I Can't Swim!

"Here we are!" Sam called out to the excited group in her mom's van. "Beautiful Lucky Lake!"

Mrs. Pearson eased off the highway into the parking lot. Just beyond, the wide lake shimmered under the late August sun. Stately pines and weeping willows lined the shore. The Lucky Lake park ranger waved to them from his cabin porch. How great to have this fantastic lake so near her home in Circleville!

"It's so nice that he gets to live here with his kids," said Sam as she waved back. "Just think, they can go hiking and swimming every day if they want. I'd love that!"

When she saw the lake, Sam's little cousin Suzie squealed. "Can Petie and I go swimming now, Aunt Jean? Please, please, please?"

"Not me," Sam's little brother, Petie, shot back. "I'm gonna eat first."

Mrs. Pearson laughed. "Petie's right, Suzie. Let's have lunch first. I need everyone's help to haul our food and stuff over to the picnic area. I'll carry the birthday cake."

My birthday cake, Sam thought with a smile. Everything had seemed so perfect for this wonderful August birthday. A perfect place: the small, but beautiful, lake just outside of town. A perfect age: 12 at last! Perfect activities: swimming, volleyball, boating. Perfect company: her family and her three PTs, Sara Fields, Le Tran and LaToya Thomas.

Yes, perfect. Then her Mom had ruined it all by inviting Suzie along!

"But she's family, Sam," Mrs. Pearson had explained. "Uncle Todd and Aunt Caitlin have to go out of town this weekend. I know Suzie's a handful sometimes, but she's lonely and needs friends. Her family aren't Christians, remember. They all need to know God's love."

A few minutes later the van was unpacked. Their arms full, Sam and her friends hurried along the trail to the picnic grounds. Up ahead, a pillar of smoke rose from the fire her dad already had going in the grill. "That Suzie!" Sam muttered. "She's just a spoiled brat!"

Sara laughed. "Oh, Sam. Don't call her that! She's just a little kid."

"Well, my brother Petie's just a little kid, too, but he's fun. She's a brat, and she's never going to change!"

"Sam," added LaToya, "remember our Bible story last Sunday? How Jesus raised Jairus' little girl from the dead? Well, nothing's hopeless with God. He can do anything."

Sam made a face. She wasn't in the mood for a Bible lesson. "Even help Suzie be nicer and not ruin my birthday?"

"Yeah, if we pray and ask Him about it."

Just then they reached Sam's dad. "The fire's just about ready, folks!" he announced. "Who wants to be Grill Sergeant?"

"Le and I do!" Sam called.

Suzie frowned. "You mean we have to wait for the food to cook? Forget it! I want to go swimming now."

"No, Suzie," Mrs. Pearson replied. "No one can go out in the lake alone, not even along the shore. The water is much too dangerous for that. We'll all eat together and Sam will open her presents. Then we'll all play in the water together. Everyone needs to have a water buddy at all times."

"Hey, Suzie," Mr. Pearson called, "want to come exploring with me and Petie? We're going to look for frogs."

Sara smiled and pointed at the trees. "Or you can go with LaToya and me. We're going to find sticks for roasting marshmallows."

Suzie stuck out her tongue. "Frogs? Sticks? Yuck! Forget it!"

As Mr. Pearson, Petie, LaToya and Sara hurried off, Sam grabbed a package of hot dogs and emptied them onto the grill. She took a deep whiff of the sweet lake air. Pine trees! Honeysuckle! Sweet clover!

Ummm! she thought.

All summer Sam had been looking forward to her birthday. Most of her friends had their birthday parties at swimming pools or restaurants or skating rinks. But Sam wanted hers to be by the lake. *Nothing is as wonderful as being in God's great outdoors*, she thought, *even with bothersome little cousins around.*

Le got out the buns and mustard while Sam turned the sizzling wieners. "Umm! Smells great!" Le exclaimed. But Suzie just grumped, "You'd better not burn mine!"

Just then, Sara and LaToya popped out of the bushes. "Marshmallow sticks!" Sara exclaimed as she waved them around.

Sam laughed. "You found some sticker bushes, too, didn't you? Look at your jeans!"

"Sticker bushes!" snickered Suzie. "Boy, that was dumb!"

Mrs. Pearson frowned. "Suzie, that's not nice."

"I don't care." Suzie kicked the picnic table. "This is boring. I'm gonna go find Petie and Uncle Joe."

Mrs. Pearson frowned. "You might get lost, Suzie. This is a big place."

"It's OK, Mrs. Pearson," Sara said, and then she pointed. "They're just on the other side of that big willow tree, right past that old boat and those blackberry bushes. You can't miss them, Suzie. Listen, you can even hear them from here."

As Suzie skipped off, the girls finished setting out all the food, including the delicious, double-chocolate birthday cake.

"Lunch time!" Sam's mom called a few minutes later. "Sam, go call the others, please."

Sam hurried down the path, calling as she ran, "Come on, everybody! Time to eat!"

"Coming, birthday girl!" her dad shouted back. In a moment he and Petie appeared around the old willow. Petie held a very unhappy frog. "Got me a new pet, Sam. Isn't he cute? Want to pet him?"

She laughed. "Later. Where's Suzie?"

Mr. Pearson stared at her. "What do you mean? Isn't she with the rest of you?"

Suddenly they heard a scream from out in the middle of the lake. It was Suzie!

The old boat was upside-down beside her. She had taken it out on the lake alone.

The little girl thrashed wildly in the choppy water "Hellllllp!" she shrieked. "I can't swim!"

"I'm coming, Suzie!" Mr. Pearson shouted back. He quickly stripped to his swim trunks. "Petie, you go with Sam. Sam, tell your mother, then run on to the park ranger for help. And pray!" Then he dove in.

After leaving Petie with her mom, Sam ran all the way to the ranger station. At first, she was angry. *Suzie has ruined my birthday*, she thought. *Serves the brat right for doing such a dumb thing!*

But the more Sam thought about it, the more ashamed she got. After she alerted the park ranger, Sam walked back to the picnic site. As she walked, she decided that instead of blaming Suzie, she would pray for her cousin to be saved from harm, just as Jesus had saved Jairus' little girl in that Bible story LaToya had mentioned earlier. Then Sam asked God to forgive her for being so selfish and critical about Suzie, and to help her show her little cousin His great love.

Later, when Sam's father and the ranger rowed back with a sobbing, shivering Suzie, everyone cheered and hugged Suzie and thanked God for saving her. The ranger's little girl lent Suzie some dry clothes. Then the park ranger's family joined them in their birthday picnic. Sam even let Suzie help her blow out her candles.

"Now Petie and I will help you open your presents, Sam!" Suzie shouted.

Sam gave her a hug. "OK. You're the boss!"

But she'd already had the best present of all —

her little cousin was safe and sound, and her own attitude and heart had changed.

· Good News · from God's Word

Sam thought of this Bible story when her little cousin was in danger. Read it and find out why.

Jairus' Daughter's Healing

FROM LUKE 8:40-42, 49-56

Jairus was a very important man. He was very busy with his business and with his synagogue. (A synagogue is a place to worship God.) Jairus was in charge of seeing that the synagogue had everything it needed to run smoothly.

But on this particular day he couldn't keep his

mind on his duties. His little girl, who was 12, was very sick. He loved her more than anything in the world. None of the doctors could help her. What in the world could he do?

Then he remembered: Jesus could help her! So he ran all the way until he found Jesus, and fell at His feet. "Master, please help me," he sobbed, "before my little girl dies."

But on their way to Jairus' home, one of his servants met them. "It's too late, sir," he said. "Your little girl is already dead."

"Don't be afraid," Jesus told Jairus. "Just believe, and she will be healed."

By the time they reached Jairus' house, it was filled with weeping people. "Stop crying," Jesus said, because He knew she would be alive again and there would be no need for tears. Then He went into the little girl's bedroom. How still she lay! But Jesus took her by the hand. "Get up, My child!" He said. Right then, she came alive again, and stood up!

Now they knew that Jesus was the Son of God. Only God can raise someone from the dead.

A Verse to Remember

God is our refuge and strength,
an ever-present help in trouble.

— Psalm 46:1

What About You?

1. Who helped little Suzie when she was in trouble? (*check all the right answers*)

   Sam ____ Sam's dad ____

   the park ranger ___ Petie ____

   the ranger's wife ____ God ____

2. Now, what about YOU? Do you really believe that God wants to help you? ______

3. Do you believe that He is able to do whatever is needed to help you? ______

4. Is there something for which you need God's help? Maybe someone you love needs healing. Maybe one of your parents is worried about a job. Or are you afraid of something? If you need God's help, write your need here:

   ____

   ____

   Do you believe God can help this prayer come true if it is His will? If so, pray about it right now. Then sign your name and today's date. And keep praying about it!

Name: ________________________

Date: ________________________

A Sinking Feeling Maze

Follow the maze below to help Sam run to the ranger's station to rescue her little cousin, Suzie. Check your solution on page 201.

Chapter 2

Clueless in Circleville

The next Sunday morning at church, the PTs could hardly wait for their Sunday school class to begin. "Oh, Miss Kotter!" Sam said to their teacher. "I wish you could have been at my birthday party! You won't believe what happened!"

"It was awesome!" LaToya echoed. "It was like being in a movie!"

Then the girls told about the birthday picnic and how little Suzie almost drowned.

"I mean, at first I was mad at her for breaking the rules," Sam confessed. "Then I was ashamed of myself and scared for her. But LaToya reminded me how Jesus brought Jairus' daughter back alive. So I prayed as hard as I could, and asked God to save little Suzie."

"And He did!" Sara added. "Sam's dad swam out to get her, then the park ranger sped out in his boat and brought them both back."

"Then we had the cake and presents and everything," Le said. "Sam even got the new basketball she wanted. And a gift certificate for the Midway Mall!"

Sam blushed. "All summer I thought I wanted that more than anything. I mean, new school clothes would be really great. And it's so much fun to shop! But then I thought Suzie might die. And, well, what I really wanted more than anything was for her to not die. And God did save her."

Miss Kotter gave Sam a hug. "Happy birthday, Sam. Our God is an awesome God, isn't He? And I'm glad you saw for yourself how He answers prayer. Today we're going to talk about someone else who prayed to God for what she wanted and how God answered that prayer." Then Miss Kotter told the Bible story of Hannah.

After that, the girls discussed what they would like to have more than anything else. Sara had her heart set on being a Madison Middle School cheerleader. Le wanted her mother to quit grieving over her father's death. LaToya longed for guitar lessons. "I want Suzie's family to get to know God," Sam decided. "I want her to know God loves her."

"What about you, Miss Kotter?" Sara asked. "What do you want most of all? For your boyfriend, Bob, to come home soon so you can get married?" Bob, who was in the Navy, had been at sea for almost a year now.

Their teacher laughed. "Well, girls, that would be wonderful. But he can't be here for several more months. And you know something? What I want for my birthday now isn't the same as what I wanted at your age. You see, my parents died when I was very young, and I had to live in an orphanage. On every birthday I would ask God to give me a real party and real parents. At the orphanage we got cake for our birthdays, but not any real presents.

"Yet during those years I learned to love the orphanage director, who we called 'Ma Jones,' very much. And now I see God did answer my prayer. Ma Jones now lives near Circleville at the Whispering Pines Nursing Home. She's old and not well. But she is still the most wonderful 'mother' God could give any little girl."

The PTs all looked at each other with surprise. "Wow!" Sara said quietly.

"But wouldn't you like some kind of present?" Le asked. "I mean, when your birthday comes, what do you want someone to give you?"

Miss Kotter thought a moment. "OK, tell you what. Since I design computer games at work, why don't we make a game of this? We'll call our puzzle the Secret Birthday Circle."

She drew a small circle in the middle of the chalkboard. "OK, what was today's Bible lesson about?"

"Prayer!"

"Praying!" "Hannah!" everyone shouted at once.

Miss Kotter drew a big "P" in the middle of the circle. "Right. This 'P' is for 'praying.' Remember that praying is simply talking to God, your loving heavenly Father. You can pray when you're in trouble, sick or worried. But you can also pray when you're happy. Every day you should praise God and thank Him for what He's done for you.

"So 'P' for 'praying' is the first Secret Letter of the Secret Birthday Circle. Each week between now and my birthday, I'll give you another Secret Letter to add to it. They will all be about Christian values, the way God wants us to live. By December 8th, when it really is my birthday, you can put all the secret letters together to find out what I want more than anything else in the world!"

Then she laughed. "Of course, sharp as you

girls are, you probably will have guessed it long before we get to the end!"

Sam was especially intrigued. She couldn't resist a good puzzle. "But what if we don't guess?" she asked. "What if we don't know what to get you for your birthday?"

Sara waved her hand. "I know!" she grinned. "We'll all pray about it, right?"

· Good News · from God's Word

Sometimes we make our prayers as short and quick as possible so we can get on with the "fun stuff" of life. This story is about a woman who put her whole heart into praying because she believed God would answer her. And He did!

Hannah's Prayer

FROM 1 SAMUEL 1:1-20

Hannah had a very happy, loving husband and lots of happy, loving relatives. But she wasn't happy herself. She longed to have a child of her own. Day after day, year after year, she prayed and asked God for a baby. But she still didn't have one.

In those days, there was just one place to worship God. This was in the tent tabernacle Moses had made for God years before. Hannah's family lived so far away from the tabernacle they could go only once a year. Hannah loved to go to God's house. But it made her sad as well. She knew God could answer prayer. He knew she wanted a little baby of her own. If God really loved her, why didn't He give her a baby?

One time, when Hannah was worshipping at the tabernacle, she felt so bad about her childlessness that she began crying and praying all at once. "Dear God," she prayed out loud, "if you'll just give me a little boy, I will give him back to You to serve You all his life."

When Eli, the priest, saw her, at first he thought something was wrong with her. *Maybe she is drunk,* he thought. But when he discovered that she was praying, Eli felt sorry for her. "Go in peace," he said. "May God give you what you asked of Him."

God did answer Hannah's prayer. He gave her a little boy named Samuel. How she praised and thanked God for her baby! She kept her promise to God, too. She gave her little boy back to God to serve

Him. When Samuel grew up, he became a great prophet for God and God's people.

A Verse to Remember

In everything, by prayer and petition, with thanksgiving, present your requests to God.

— Philippians 4:6

What About You?

Look back to the end of Chapter 1. What needs did you write for God's help? Are you still praying for them? Maybe there is something else you want to pray about. Maybe, like Hannah, there's something you want more than anything else in the world. Maybe it's a new bike for school. Or a ride to church every week. Or to do well in school. Or for your parents to become Christians. Whatever it is that you want to pray about, write it on the lines below.

What I want more than anything in the world:

____

____

Next, unscramble these letters to show what Hannah did about something she wanted very much:

EHS YEARPD OT DGO

Write your answer here:

____

Now pray about your request, just as Hannah did.

A "Prayer Is" Quiz

Here's an easy quiz about prayer. Find the rhyming word from the list below to fill each blank.

A. hands
B. pray
C. bless
D. eyes
E. indeed
F. to
G. know
H. me

1. When she prays, Sam always tries
   To bow her head and close her ____.
2. It also helps, she understands,
   To sit quite still and fold her ____.
3. We all should talk to God each day
   And in the name of Jesus _____.
4. We can tell God what we need
   Because He loves us much, ____.
5. We must believe that God can do
   Everything we ask Him ____.
6. When we talk to God, you see,
   We know He hears both you and ____.
7. His answer may be "no" or "yes"
   Or "wait," but He will always ____.
8. And as we see the blessings flow,
   We should show our thanks to Him, we ____.

For the answers to What About You? and A "Prayer Is" Quiz, see page 201.

Chapter 3

Now What Do I Say?

"What a drag!" Sam mumbled to herself as she dressed for church the following Sunday morning. "Tomorrow's Labor Day, and I have to spend it all by myself!"

It was the very last weekend of summer. Sure, she'd be with her PTs this morning at church. And she'd be with them Tuesday as they all headed back to Madison Middle School for the new school year. But for the big holiday in between, the other three girls were having family get-togethers. Without her.

When Sam complained to her mom that she didn't want to be alone on Labor Day, her mom laughed. "You know you won't be alone tomorrow," she said. "Uncle Todd, Aunt Caitlin and Suzie are coming over. We're having burgers and watermelon and homemade ice cream. And you know Uncle Todd loves basketball. Maybe he'll shoot some baskets with you.

"By the way, I noticed the 'For Sale' sign next door has come down. Maybe one of our new neighbors will be a girl your age!"

"Maybe," Sam sighed. She really wanted to be with her PTs, not some new girl. But at least her Uncle Todd and Aunt Caitlin were coming over. Maybe this time she could talk to them about Jesus.

That morning in Sunday school, Miss Kotter began by talking about friends, neighbors and strangers. "We're getting new neighbors," Sam said. "But I don't know if I'll like them or not. It's much more fun to be with people I already know, like all of you."

"What do the rest of you think about that?" their teacher asked.

"Well, I used to be a stranger," Le said. "When I first moved here I didn't know anyone. But one day LaToya and I just started talking at our lockers after school. We laughed about both of us wearing ponytails. And then the rest of you started being nice to me, too, and invited me to church and parties and everything. And next thing I knew, we were all best friends."

Miss Kotter smiled. "Do you know Rebekah faced a similar problem? She had to decide the proper way to treat someone she didn't know: ignore him, be mean to him or be kind and helpful. Why don't we see what she decided?"

After Miss Kotter told the Bible story, Sam raised her hand. "Rebekah decided to be kind and neighborly, even if it was easier not to be. "

"That way she made a new friend," LaToya added.

Sara nodded. "I always try to remember that Jesus said to love our neighbors as ourselves. I try to treat others the way I want to be treated, but it's not always easy, especially when my big brother, Tony, bugs me."

"Good!" Miss Kotter smiled, pleased that they understood the lesson. "Now we can add this week's Secret Letter to our Secret Birthday Circle. It's 'N' — for 'neighborly.' " Miss Kotter wrote an "N" in the blank #4 section of the large circle on her chalkboard. "God wants us to be kind and loving to everyone."

Le grinned. "Just the way Sam's going to be to her new neighbors! Especially if they're all basketball stars!"

The next morning, the sun rose hot and bright. "Going to be a scorcher!" Mr. Pearson remarked. "Over 100 degrees in the shade. Sam, do you want to help me set up our wading pool for Suzie and Petie?"

"OK," she grinned. "But only if you promise not to let Suzie get near a boat this time!"

As Sam and her dad filled the pool out back, she suddenly heard a truck motor — and lots of noise and talking. Petie rushed out to the backyard. "Sam, guess what?"

"Are Uncle Todd and Aunt Caitlin here?"

"Yeah. But that's not all. Our new neighbors are moving in. And they have kids!" He raced out front again.

Sam raced out, too.

People and furniture seemed to be everywhere. So did dark-haired, smiling children. Petie and Suzie were right in the middle of them.

"Sam!" Petie called excitedly. "These guys are twins, Ricardo and Juan. Can they come in the pool with us?"

Suzie grabbed the hand of a shy little girl. "This is Lolita. I'm going to teach her how to swim."

Sam giggled to think of Suzie teaching anyone to swim. Just then a girl came out of the house carrying empty boxes. A tall girl, just about Sam's age. She had a ponytail, too. A long, wavy brown one.

"Hi!" Sam called.

"*Buenos dias*!" the new girl called back.

Suddenly Sam felt very strange. *Oh, no!* she

thought. *These new neighbors don't even speak English! Maybe they are from a different country. How can I be friends with people I don't understand? Maybe I'd better just go back inside and forget this.*

Then she remembered Rebekah and her kindness to strangers. "*Buenos dias*!" she tried to say, but it came out more like "boonas days."

Her new neighbor giggled. "Hey, not bad. I'm Maria Moreno. My mom wants me to round up these kids and get them out of the movers' way. Want to help?"

She did speak English! "Uh, hi. I'm Sam Pearson. I just filled our wading pool in the backyard. We can take the kids over there to play, if it's OK with your mom."

What a Labor Day that turned out to be! After the moving van was finally empty, the Pearsons and the Morenos held a big party that stretched across both backyards. Even the movers were invited! The Pearsons brought hamburgers, hot dogs, watermelon, potato salad, hand-cranked ice cream and Mrs. Pearson's double-chocolate cake. Mrs. Moreno added her delicious tacos and chicken burritos. It was truly a feast!

Aunt Caitlin remembered some of the Spanish she had learned in college, so she and Mrs. Moreno were soon sharing recipes and jokes. Uncle Todd shot baskets with Sam — and with Maria, too. Maria was almost better than Sam! After they sat down in the grass to catch their breath and guzzle some lemonade, Sam found the right moment to tell Uncle Todd that

Jesus was her best friend. He listened quietly as she explained her faith. She was scared to do it, but afterward she was so glad she had.

Then Sam told Maria all about the PTs and Faith Church and Madison Middle School.

That night after everyone had gone home, Sam went to her room and laid out her new school supplies and clothes for the next day. She realized that she had had a great time that day even though she missed her PTs, and it was all because she showed kindness to a stranger.

Sam's mom came in the room.

"Well, Sam," her mom said, smiling, "this day wasn't nearly as lonely as you thought it would be, was it?"

"You know, Mom," Sam said, "I'm sure glad God invented neighbors!"

· Good News · From God's Word

Someone once said, "A stranger is a friend you just haven't met yet." What would Sam have missed if she hadn't been friendly to Maria? In this Bible story, see what Rebekah would have missed if she hadn't been kind to someone new.

Rebekah's Kindness

From Genesis 24:1-32

Rebekah was a beautiful young woman who loved being around animals. She especially loved her family's camels. She noticed that they worked so hard and they were graceful when carrying large loads across the desert. Camels could get very angry if people were mean to them. Sometimes it took several strong men to calm an angry camel. But Rebekah was always kind and gentle to them. They followed her around like happy puppy dogs.

One difficult part of taking care of the camels was watering them. Camels could go for days in the desert without water, but that meant drinking lots and lots of water ahead of time.

Guess who had to haul the water for them? Rebekah! Not with a faucet and hose, but by dipping a big, heavy jar down a well, and drawing it up. It took many jars full of water to make all her camels happy.

One day when Rebekah came to the well, she saw a stranger there with a lot of his own camels. He looked very tired and thirsty. His poor camels looked tired and thirsty, too. The man didn't have a jar to draw water from the well.

"Please!" he cried to Rebekah when he saw her jar. "Could I have just a little drink?"

"Of course!" Rebekah replied. She let him drink all he wanted. After that, she could have gone ahead and watered her own camels, but instead, she said, "Let me water your camels for you. They're so hot and thirsty."

Watering twice as many animals meant working twice as hard. But Rebekah had a kind heart and wanted to help this tired, thirsty man.

The man was Abraham's servant. He saw that Rebekah was as beautiful as she was kind. God showed him that this kind woman would make a wonderful wife for Abraham's son Isaac. Rebekah became Isaac's beautiful bride!

So be nice to strangers and show God's love. You never know what might happen!

A Verse to Remember

Do not forget to entertain strangers.

— Hebrews 13:2

What About You?

1. Which of your neighbors do you like best?

    ____

2. Which do you like the least? ____________________

3. Does God say it's OK to not be nice to the ones you don't like? _______

4. What about at school? Should you be nice to all the kids, or just to the most popular ones?

    ____

The Secret Birthday Circle

The Secret Birthday Circle Miss Kotter drew for the PTs is on the next page. Print a "P" for "praying" in the center circle. This was the Secret Letter you learned in Chapter 2. Then write an "N" for "neighborly" in space 4 for this chapter's Secret Letter.

As you continue through the book, return to page 44 to write each of the other Secret Letters as you discover them. See if you can guess what the circle will read when it's completed!

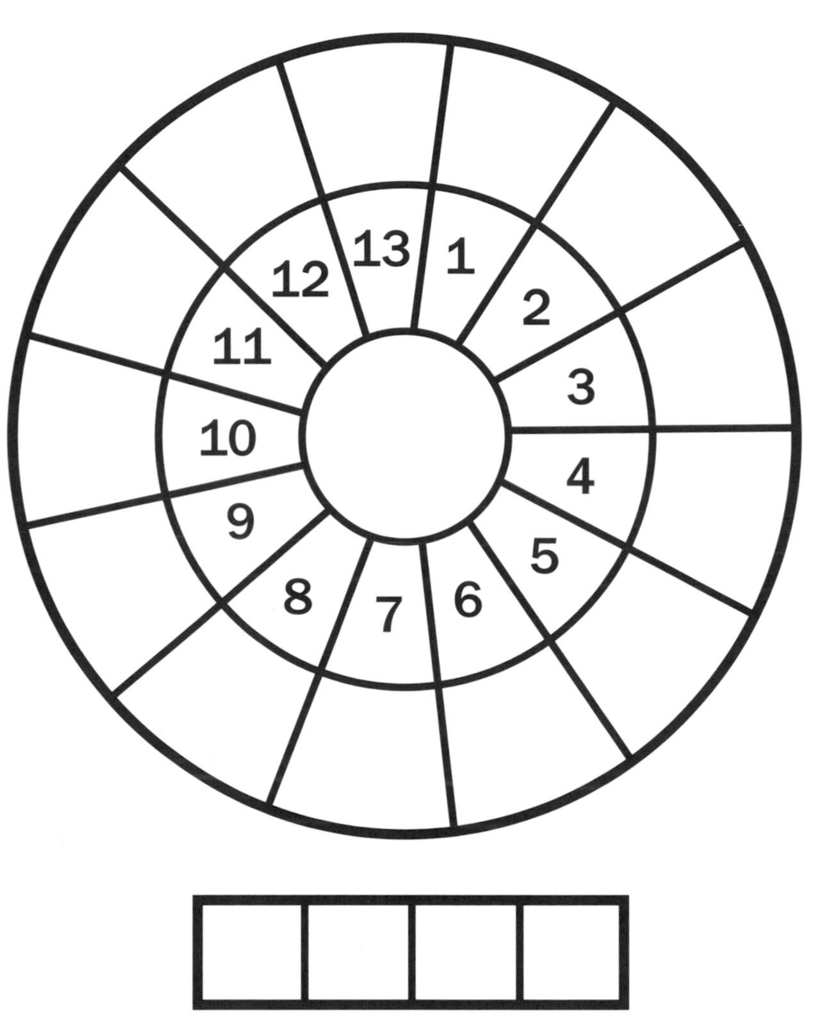
13
1
12
2
11
3
10
4
9
5
8
7
6

Chapter 4

Try, Try Again

The first week of school was awesome. The second was even better!

Sam signed up as a volunteer for Mr. Pilanto, the Madison basketball coach. Le went out for girls' soccer. Maria aced her first science test. Sara met some of the cheerleading squad. LaToya enrolled in guitar lessons.

And that Friday night, Pastor Andy and all of the Faith Church youth groups from Zone 56 up through college-age sponsored a big praise night with a visiting band.

"I wish all the kids at our school were here tonight," Sam whispered to Sara during a quiet moment in the service.

"Well, did you invite any of them?" Sara whispered back.

The girls looked at each other with big eyes. They'd put up posters and handed out notices. But they never actually invited anyone personally at school. They had just hoped their friends would show up.

While they waited for their parents to pick them up from the church, the PTs talked about how they could get more people to come to church.

That night, Le thought about it some more. Then she called Sam.

"Sam," Le said, "what if you and I go door-to-door in our neighborhood tomorrow and personally invite people to church?"

"Sounds great," Sam agreed. "If we ride our bikes, we can swing by the church and pick up some bulletins to give to people. I can finish my chores and be at your house by 10 if Mom says it's OK. What about you?"

"I'll check with my mom and call you back."

As Le entered the living room, she passed a hall shrine with flickering candles and incense. In the middle was a picture of her late father. A great sadness filled Le's heart. *I miss you, Dad,* Le thought, *every single day. But I know I'll be with you again in heaven. I wish Mom knew that, too. Then maybe she wouldn't be so sad.*

Le's mother, a well-known concert pianist, still grieved daily for her husband. Daniel Tran became a Christian after he married her. But Mrs. Tran stayed a Buddhist, just as she had been back in Vietnam. "Christians are good people," she would say. "Buddhists are good people, too. So why should I change?"

As Le entered the room her mother sat motionless at their grand piano, staring silently out the window.

"Mom," Le asked gently, "is it all right for Sam and me to take some church fliers door-to-door in our neighborhood tomorrow?"

"Tomorrow?" her mother exploded. "Le, you know good and well I have a big concert tomorrow afternoon. I need you to vacuum and dust and clean up for me while I'm gone. Remember, we're having company for dinner."

Le swallowed hard. "I'll clean everything, Mom. I promise."

"You tell me Christians always keep their promises. Well, let's see if you can keep that one!"

The next morning, Sam arrived just as Mrs. Tran left. Sam held out a bag to Le. "I brought some colored paper and markers. We can make and fold little invitations to hand to people along with the bulletins."

"Then let's get started," Le answered. "We'll have to work fast to do all this and still get back in time for me to clean the house before my mom gets back."

"Don't worry," Sam said. "I'll help you."

When the invitations were finished, the girls stopped by Faith Church. Pastor McConahan was just setting out the next day's bulletins. He read over Sam and Le's invitations, then prayed with the girls that God would bless what they were going to do.

"Smile and be courteous," he instructed them. "Let everyone who sees you see the love of Jesus."

Their smiles were dazzling when they knocked on the first door. But no one was home. Leaving an invitation and bulletin on the doorstep, they hurried on to the next house.

There, a big dog growled right inside the door. Someone yelled, "Go away. We don't want any." At the third house, children begged them for free candy. And their dogs kept jumping up on Sam and Le, trying to lick their faces.

The two girls went up and down the streets. Some people were home, some weren't. They left invitations and bulletins at each home. But no one said, "Yes, we'll come to your church."

Back at Le's house, the girls were discouraged. "I thought God would make this work better," Le sighed. "You know, the way He blessed Dorcas."

The Sunday before, their Sunday school class had studied Dorcas. Miss Kotter explained that Dorcas was always diligent about doing good, and that "diligent" meant to keep trying, even when things weren't easy. Miss Kotter had marked a big "D" in the #13 section of the Secret Birthday Circle — as in "D" for "diligent."

"I know," Le replied. "We did our best. But it looks as though our best wasn't good enough. No one in our neighborhood wants to come to church."

Then she smiled. "Hey, I just remembered. We haven't asked my mom yet. Want to help me get her invitation ready?"

Later that afternoon when Mrs. Tran returned home, she could hardly believe her eyes. "Everything looks so wonderful!" she cried. "Even fresh flowers!"

"Thank you, Mom," Le said. "We did this as a happy way to welcome you home. And to invite you to come to church with us tomorrow." Then she handed her mother a little invitation and bulletin.

Mrs. Tran started to cry. Then she wiped her eyes. "Church? We'll see. But thank you, girls. Now I need to start dinner."

Sam and Le smiled. God had blessed their efforts for Him after all!

· Good News · From God's Word

Sam and Le were reminded of this story when they thought of doing good for God.

Dorcas' Good Deeds

FROM ACTS 9:36-41

As Jesus' friend Peter traveled around helping the Christians, he met a wonderful woman named Dorcas. She was always helping poor people and doing other good things. She made clothes for children and adults — and then gave them away with a smile and a hug. No one could say one bad thing about Dorcas!

But then one day a very sad thing happened. Dorcas suddenly became very ill and died. "Run and tell Peter!" cried her friends.

Peter rushed to Dorcas' house. It was full of crying people showing off all the lovely clothes Dorcas had made for them. Peter sent everyone out of the room. He got down on his knees and prayed, asking God for help. Then he told Dorcas to get up.

Just like that, she opened her eyes and sat up! It was a miracle! Dorcas really had been dead, but God made her alive again. How glad all the people were. Dorcas was glad, too. Now she could keep on helping all her friends!

A Verse to Remember

Show this same diligence to the very end.

— Hebrew 6:11

You Are Invited!

Would you like to invite people to your church? You can make an invitation to hand to your friends or neighbors like Sam and Le did. If you have a computer, you can design an invitation on it using special software and paper. You can also buy cards that have lovely pictures on the outside and blank areas inside for you to write on.

Or, fold a piece of paper (colored is nice) in half, then in half again. Now it should look like a greeting card. On the front, write or print "You Are Invited." Draw some pictures or add attractive stickers. Designs relating to the time of year are always a good idea. You can also use the leaf and flower patterns on the next page. Trace and color them, then cut them out. For fall, color the leaves yellow, gold, red, or brown. For spring and summer, color them in shades of green.

Inside your card, print "To my church." Then write your church's name and address. If you are not sure how to spell something, ask someone who knows or take a peek at your church's newsletter or bulletin. When you are ready to deliver the invitation, ask someone to go with you, just to be safe. Be sure to wear smiles!

Secret Letter

Turn to the Secret Birthday Circle on page 44. Add a "D" for "diligent" to space 13.

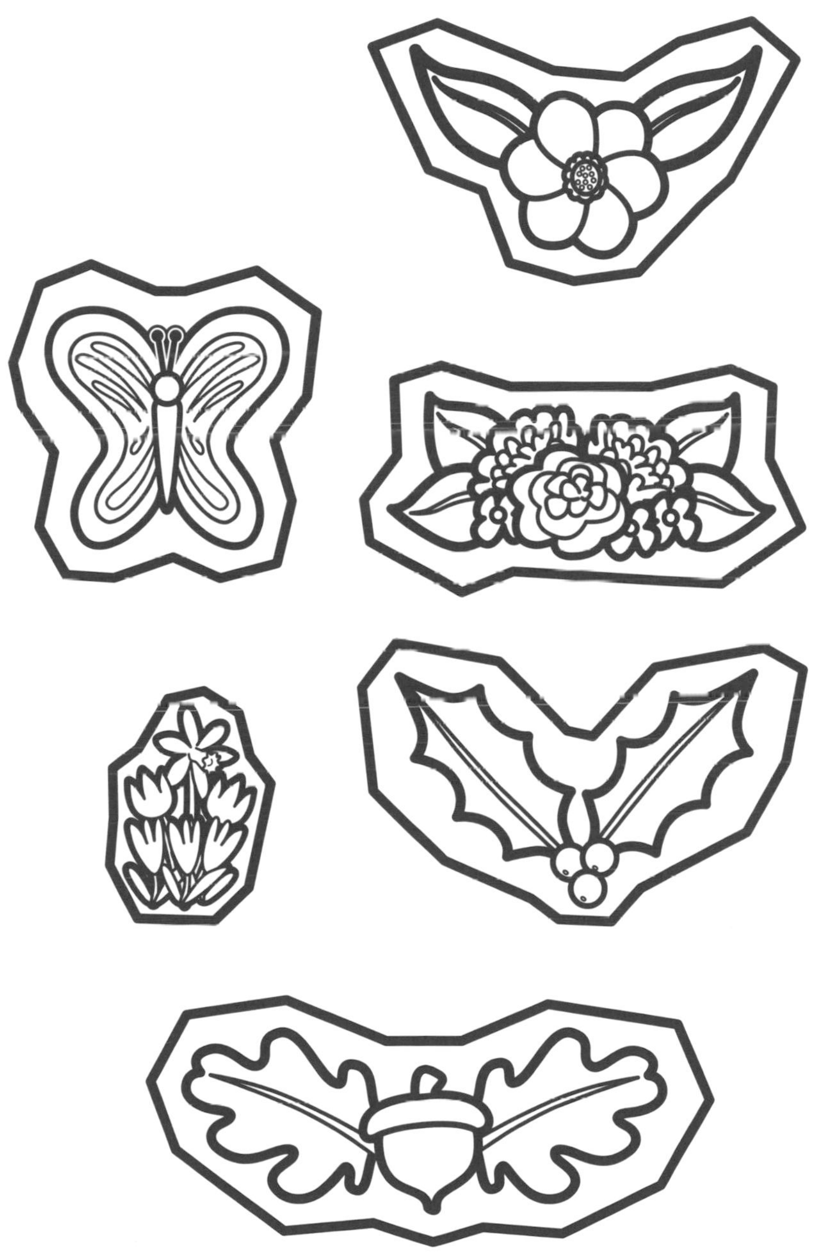

Chapter 5

Obey? No Way!

That Friday afternoon at school, Sam stared at the writing on the chalkboard. "Uh, Mr. Talley, I think you made a mistake. That big assignment you have up there called 'Something I Can Do to Improve My World'? It says it's due in just two weeks. Don't you mean it's due at the end of the semester?"

Her teacher looked up, frowning. "No, I don't, young lady." As the class groaned, he said, "Each team's report is due exactly two weeks from today. So you'll need to pick your teammate and get going. I want your best work — not something you scribble out the night before or pull off the Internet. You can include pictures and charts. But I want everything to be what you learned on your own."

"Oh, Sara," Sam said after class, "I'm so glad you and I could team up. It would take me two whole weeks just to pick a subject by myself. I mean, what is something I can do to improve my world?"

"Do away with homework?" Sara joked. "At least we have the weekend to think up ideas."

That evening when Sam's mom came home from her job at the Paws and Pooches Animal Shelter, she was all excited. "We need to raise money to help feed more animals this winter," she said. "So we're going to hold an animal fair a week from Saturday. We're planning things like a teddy bear contest, pet parade, dog obedience class, pet clinic, donkey rides and more! It's going to be right downtown at Shawnee Park. One of the TV stations is even sponsoring it all!"

Sam smiled. *Hmmm,* she thought. *Maybe we could write our paper on saving animals from hunger and cold weather. Sara would love that.*

"Can I bring Sneezit?" Petie asked, grabbing the tiny dog up into his arms. "Maybe he'll win for the smallest."

"Good idea, Petie," Sam replied. "You can show him off in the pet parade. Then I'll take him to the dog obedience class. It would be nice to finally get him trained." Sam was thinking she could write about the dog class for her project, too.

After dinner, Sam called Sara and told her the news. "Think we could do our project on it? Our topic could be 'Helping Our Animal Friends.' You could write about feeding and protecting them. I'll write about how pets need to learn to obey. We can both take pictures at the shelter and at the fair. The TV station is going to be there, too. Maybe we'll even be on the news!"

"Let's do it!" Sara cried. "Let's ask your mom if she can take us to the shelter so we can start tomorrow."

The next morning, Mrs. Pearson drove the girls to the shelter. "Oh, Sam, I'm so glad you came along to help me," her mother said. "I have so much to do today to get ready for the fair." But every time Mrs. Pearson asked Sam to do something, Sam ran off to take another picture.

Sunday morning in Sunday school class, Miss Kotter looked around as she greeted everyone.

"Welcome, Maria!" she said. "We're so glad you're going to be in our class from now on. But where is Le?"

LaToya smiled. "She'll be here later for church, Miss Kotter. She wanted to wait until later so she could come with her mom. She's coming with her today for the very first time! Le was a good witness just by keeping her promises to her."

Miss Kotter clapped her hands together. "How wonderful! See how God answers prayer? But along with our prayers He wants our obedience." Then she told the Bible story of Sarah and her trusting obedience to God. After the lesson, she wrote an "O" for "obedience" in the Secret Birthday Circle at space 6.

But Sam wasn't really paying attention. She was thinking of the dog obedience class at the fair, and how much easier life would be when little Sneezit learned to obey.

All week long, Mrs. Pearson worked extra hard at both the shelter and at home. But whenever she asked Sam to help her, Sam would say, "I can't. I've got to work on my social studies project with Sara." Every day, Sara did work on their project. But Sam just kept goofing off.

Finally, the day before the animal fair, Sam's mom came down with the flu. "She's just been working too hard," the doctor said. "She's going to have to stay in bed a few days."

So Mrs. Pearson didn't get to go to the fair after all. Sara's mom took Sara and Sam, along with Sara's Great Dane, Tank, and Sam's tiny dog, Sneezit. Mrs. Fields, an artist, did sketches of people's pets at the fair. Sam spent the day babysitting Petie and trying to help with the booths. She never even got near the dog obedience class.

It was as if Sam needed an obedience class herself. She hadn't obeyed God's Word, or her mother. She'd taken the easy way out and let her mom do all the hard work by herself. Now her poor mother was sick. And it was all Sam's fault.

"I'm sorry, God," Sam confessed when she realized how wrong she had been. "Please forgive me and help me do better."

The following Friday when the social studies teams gave their reports, Sara and Sam presented a slide show of all the pictures they took at the shelter and fair. Then Sara gave her report on taking care of animals as a way to improve the world. Next it was Sam's turn.

"For people and animals to live together happily," she said, "animals usually need to follow certain rules. That's why we have obedience classes for our dogs, so they won't hurt people or other pets or themselves.

"People need to obey rules, too. We need to obey our teachers, our parents, the government's laws and God's laws. I could have had a lot better report to give you today if I had obeyed my mother. Instead, I made her sick.

"So what can I do to improve my world? Be nicer to the people and animals all around me. Listen to what God says and do it. And obey my mom and dad!"

· Good News · From God's Word

Pets that obey rules are happier pets. Girls that obey them are happier, too — especially God's rules. See what helped Sarai be happier in this Bible story.

Sarai's Obedience to God

From Genesis 11:28-13:4

Sarai (whom God later renamed "Sarah") loved her beautiful home in Ur. This bustling city by the River Euphrates was filled with luxurious buildings, marvelous bazaars to shop in, and all kinds of trade and industry. Her husband, Abram (whom God later renamed "Abraham"), and his father, Terah, were both wealthy. Life was easy.

There was just one problem. Ur was also an evil city. Most people there worshipped idols. God wanted Sarai's family to leave that sinful place and move to Canaan. There they could worship Him and live for Him the right way.

Of course, there were no moving vans back then. Everything had to be hauled by donkeys, camels or oxen. But Sarai, Abram, Terah and the rest of their family all wanted to obey God. So they packed up and set out for Canaan.

After traveling for hundreds of miles, they came to the mountains. There they stopped to rest in the big city of Haran. Then they looked up at the mountains ahead. They were so high! It would be hard to cross them!

"You know, we've come a long way already," Terah said. "We're tired. Why go all the way to Canaan? Why not just stay and worship God here?"

And so they did. But many people in Haran worshipped idols, too. Sarai's family still had not obeyed God. They had obeyed Him by leaving Ur, but they still weren't in the place God wanted them to be.

After Terah died, God told Abram to take his family the rest of the way to Canaan. So he and Sarai packed up and went there. They traveled all over Canaan learning about their new homeland. They even went to Egypt and back. Finally, they settled down just where God wanted them to be. Today, this nation is called Israel, after one of Abram's own grandsons!

A Verse to Remember

Obey the Lord your God.

— Jeremiah 26:13

My Pet Subject

You probably have a real pet or a stuffed animal that you care for, cuddle, talk to and enjoy looking at. Write about your own "pet" or thc one you'd like to have below. Name it and draw its picture.

My Favorite Pet

is a ____________________ named

____________________.

My Times Are God's Times

Do you have regular chores, homework or other obligations like club meetings or church activities? If so, write them all on the chart on page 63, along with school (if you're not on vacation), when you need to wake up in the morning and when you need to go to bed at night. This week, see how often you do what you are supposed to do or how often you have to be reminded of your responsibilities. Ask God to help you do even better next week!

Secret Letter

Be sure to add an "O" for "obedient" to space 6 in your Secret Birthday Circle on page 44.

		SUNDAY	MONDAY	TUESDAY	WEDNESDAY	THURSDAY	FRIDAY	SATURDAY
MORNING AM	6:00							
	7:00							
	8:00							
	9:00							
	10:00							
	11:00							
AFTERNOON PM	12:00							
	1:00							
	2:00							
	3:00							
	4:00							
	5:00							
EVENING PM	6:00							
	7:00							
	8:00							
	9:00							
	10:00							

Chapter 6

Don't Leave the Leaves!

As she talked, Sam pointed her rake toward the towering maples up and down their street. "It's like living in a golden dreamworld," she told Maria. "Isn't it beautiful?"

Laughing, Maria swished her rake through a pile of shimmering leaves. "Who says money doesn't grow on trees? We're like pirates raking in treasure!"

Just then, Petie ran up with Maria's little brothers. "Can we play in the leaves yet, huh, please?"

"Not until they're in a pile first," Maria replied. "Then you guys and the dogs can play in them while we put them in trash bags."

"You know," Sam continued, "my grandma used to store leaves like this behind her house in a compost pile. I wish our back yard was big enough for that."

Maria thought a moment. "Oh, I guess that explains that house," she said as she pointed down the street. "Their yard is a mess. Do you think they are making a huge compost pile?"

Sam rolled her eyes. "Are you kidding? That house is an embarrassment to this entire street. The Greenleafs live there. Their place used to look nice but now they're too lazy to do anything. They don't even come out of their house anymore. The grass hasn't been mown in weeks! You know, when Le and I went there a few weeks ago to invite them to church, nobody would even answer the door. And I know someone was home!"

Maria started raking from a different angle. "Maybe something's wrong."

"Oh, you're right there! Being lazy *is* wrong, as far as I'm concerned!"

Finally, Sam and Maria got the last of the leaves raked into a huge pile. With running leaps, the kids and dogs plunged happily into them. Leaves flew everywhere! Then the boys helped pack the leaves in bags and sweep up the walks and driveways.

"That was fun!" Petie declared. "Wish we had

more leaves to rake up."

"Your room is such a mess," Sam teased, "you could probably use the rake in there!"

At Sunday school class the next morning, everyone had news about the past week to share. Sara was taking a training class for cheerleader tryouts. "My mom's coming to church again today!" Le reported.

LaToya was now a guitar player with the Zone 56 worship band. "And I play at home for my Granny B., too," she added. "We love to sing together."

Sam said that the animal fair made a lot of money for the animals, and that her mom was now feeling better. Maria told how happy her whole family was to live in Circleville, and what fun it was to rake leaves with Sam. "This is such a pretty neighborhood," she said. "All the yards are so well taken care of. Except for that yellow house at the end of our street."

Miss Kotter nodded. "That yellow house at the end of your street? I hear that a little old lady lives there all alone. She's in poor health and in a wheelchair. Her son used to live with her, but he was killed in a car accident last summer."

LaToya gasped. "How sad!"

Suddenly Sam felt ashamed of herself for misjudging her neighbor. "I…I'm sorry, Miss Kotter. I didn't know. Maybe we could help her."

Miss Kotter picked up her Bible. "You know, when we hear that someone is in need, there are two things we can do. We can pretend we didn't hear it and go on our way. Or we can see how God wants us to help. Today's Bible story tells about a young girl who knew someone who was in trouble, and who knew God wanted her to help."

After she told the Bible story about a little servant girl, she asked, "What Secret Letter should we put on our Secret Birthday Circle today?"

" 'H' for helpful!" the girls shouted at once. Then Maria asked, "Miss Kotter, could you go with us to visit Mrs. Greenleaf and see what we can do for her?"

"Of course! I'll call you girls this afternoon!"

When they rang Mrs. Greenleaf's doorbell, she called out, "Go away. Leave me alone. I can't buy anything." Finally, Miss Kotter talked her into coming to the door. That's when they discovered that the old woman was indeed sick and in a wheelchair. She was going blind, too. In fact, only a grocery delivery service that came by weekly had kept her from starving to death.

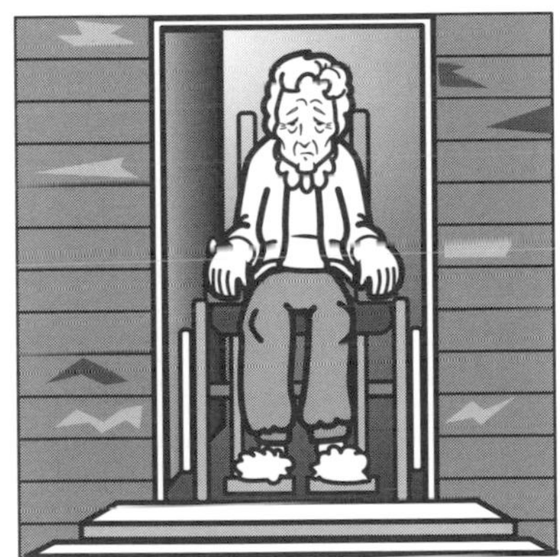

"I'm going to contact the county social services for you right away," Miss Kotter told the frail old woman. "You need a good medical checkup. And girls, look around you. How else can we help?"

That Saturday a whole army of workers and a big trash bin descended on Sam's street. All of the PTs and their families were there. So were half the people from Faith Church. Plus a lot of kids and teachers from Madison Middle School, including usually grumpy Mr. Talley, the social studies teacher, now wearing the biggest smile in the world. And they were all headed for Mrs. Greenleaf's yellow house.

All day long the volunteers worked. They painted, hammered, scrubbed, swept, mowed, pruned, polished and repaired Mrs. Greenleaf's home inside and out. The PTs did all of the raking and weeding themselves.

"Thank you, thank you!" Mrs. Greenleaf kept telling everyone. "You must really love God to be so kind to me."

When Pastor McConahan found that Mrs. Greenleaf missed going to her old church in another town, he promised to get her a ride to Faith Church the very next day. Then she cried as she told everyone, "Thank you, thank you" all over again!

Mr. Talley said "thank you," too, to Sam and her friends. "See," he explained, "how we can help 'improve the world around us' just by helping this one person in need?"

· Good News · From God's Word

Being helpful takes effort. But the PTs found out that the effort was well worth it. The girl in the following Bible story discovered the very same thing.

A Servant Girl's Advice

FROM 2 KINGS 5:1-14

It is so sad for someone to be kidnapped, stolen away from home and family, and made a slave in a far land! It's even more terrible for this to happen to someone who's very young.

But that's what happened long ago to a little girl from Israel. After she was taken away to a new land, she could have spent all her time crying and being homesick. But she believed in God and knew He loved her and would take care of her. She knew He wanted her to be kind and helpful to people wherever she lived.

Soon she was taken to the home of a great general, Naaman. She was so kind and loving to him and his wife, who did not know the true God, that Naaman began listening to her advice, even though she was just a little slave girl!

One day something terrible happened. Naaman discovered he had leprosy. In those days, there was no cure for this terrible disease that caused people to get sores all over their bodies. So nobody knew what to do for Naaman. Nobody except the little servant girl, that is.

"General Naaman should go see God's prophet Elisha," she said. "Elisha can cure him."

Naaman didn't know who Elisha was, but he hurried to his king to ask if he could go find him. "Yes!" cried his king.

Naaman went to Samaria. He was healed, and returned home rejoicing and praising the true God. But not rejoicing half as much as the little servant girl, whose faith had helped him be well again!

A Verse to Remember

We work with you for your joy.

— 2 Corinthians 1:24

What About You?

Take this true or false quiz and find out how helpful you are.

1. We should help others so we'll get praised for it.
   T __ F __

2. If my parents want me to do chores, they should pay me for it!
   T __ F __

3. A good way girls my age can help people is by babysitting. T __ F __

4. Helping is for grownups. God wants me to just play now. T __ F __

5. Girls and boys should both help their parents when they need it. T __ F __

6. Jesus is always ready to help me when I need Him.
   T __ F __

7. Helping others is one way we can show them God's love. T __ F __

8. Each time I do a good deed I get a "point" on a scorecard up in heaven. T __ F __

Check your answers on page 201.

My Good Deeds Diary

Starting today, write down each time that you help someone, along with the date that you do it. Use the space below to begin your list.

Remember to help others because you want to, not because you have to. You will be the one blessed most of all, because helping others brings you closer to God.

____

____

____

____

____

____

____

Secret Letter

Add an "H" for "helpful" in space 8 of your Secret Birthday Circle on page 44.

Chapter 7

Oh, No! Not Miss Kotter!

"Finally! At last!" Petie shouted as he ran around the yard. "It's MY birthday! I'm seven years old! I'm almost grown up!"

Petie wanted a party for his birthday but he couldn't decide what kind. At first he wanted a cartoon theme. Then an action figure one. Then sports. He couldn't decide where to have it, either. At the Paws and Pooches Shelter where he and his friends could play with all the animals? At a miniature golf course with Maria's brothers? In their back yard? On a pumpkin farm with a hayride?

Finally, he decided on an afternoon at Shawnee Park. His mom told him that was a good choice because there were lots of things to do at the park: play ball, swing, slide, eat pizza and cake, and jump around in a bounce house. Plus they would enjoy a piñata filled with candy and lots of presents, courtesy of the Morenos.

"It's been getting colder, Petie," Sam teased him. "What if it snows on your birthday?"

"Then I'll make a big fort and have a snowball fight," he giggled. But as he thought more about the possibility for snow, he became alarmed. "It won't snow, will it? Not on my birthday?"

"I hope not," Sam assured him. And indeed, when Petie's big day came at last, it was chilly, but the sky was bright and beckoning. It was all systems go!

Sam went over to the park early with her dad to take lawn chairs, hang balloons and reserve a picnic table. Petie soon arrived with their mom and all of the food. Maria brought her brothers and Lolita, while several of Petie's classmates from school came with their parents. So did Suzie with Uncle Todd and Aunt Caitlin. By noon, the bounce house was alive with children.

Later, LaToya, Le and Sara dropped by. And then Miss Kotter showed up, but she was dressed for work in a suit and heels. "I had to go to the office this morning for a big meeting," she told the PTs. "Actually, I was there most of the night, too, trying to meet a deadline. I should have gone home and changed my clothes, but I didn't want to miss anything. Especially not Petie's birthday lunch!"

After sharing some pizza and cold drinks, the younger children climbed back inside the bounce house. Sam and her PTs took a walk up a hilly trail with Miss Kotter, away from all the noise. Most of the trees in the park had lost their leaves now. The crisp, brown piles of fallen leaves crunched under their feet. Overhead, geese headed south, flying in a V-shape.

"Another fall!" sighed Miss Kotter. "How time flies. Seems like every year goes faster."

"It's hard to believe Petie is 7," Sam said. "And it's hard to believe I'm 12!"

LaToya nodded. "Sometimes I can't wait to be a teenager. But other times I want to stay a kid as long as I can. Weird, huh?"

"Not necessarily," their teacher replied. "I love being grown-up and so will you someday. It's a whole new world of jobs and travel and education and romance. But I think childhood is wonderful, too. I even enjoyed my childhood in the orphanage. Listen to the happy noises Petie's friends are making. Adults sometimes forget the sheer joy of being alive and having fun!"

Sara listened a moment. "You know, I think they've started games already. We'd better go back."

But as the group made their way to the picnic

site, Miss Kotter turned her ankle and slipped, falling several feet down the hill.

"Oh, no!" LaToya cried. "Not Miss Kotter!"

Their teacher moaned. "My ankle!"

"Don't let her stand up! I'll run for help!" Sam shouted.

"Miss Kotter's hurt!" Sam yelled as she neared Petie's party. But the younger children were having a race and screaming so loudly that no one could hear Sam. It was up to her alone to help her teacher.

Quickly, Sam scooped up a lawn chair and two brooms which were brought for a broomball game. Then she grabbed a cold can of soda and a blindfold, and rushed back to the accident scene.

Miss Kotter was sitting up now, but she was in a lot of pain. The girls helped her wrap the blindfold around her ankle for support. Then Miss Kotter held the cold can against it to keep the swelling down.

After helping their teacher up into the chair, Sam and the PTs slipped the brooms under the seat. Two girls on each side grabbed the broom handles. Another held onto the back of the seat to keep the chair from tipping over. Then they slowly carried her back to the picnic site, perched atop the chair like a queen!

But this queen wasn't feeling so royal. Trying to smile, Miss Kotter said, "When I said I loved 'fall,' this wasn't the kind of fall I meant!"

Then she added, "Thank you, girls. You are very resourceful. Our lesson in Sunday school tomorrow was supposed to be about Miriam, who was also very resourceful. But you may have to read about her yourself in your Bibles if I can't get to church.

"I should have been more resourceful in wearing proper shoes for hiking!"

As soon as Sam's dad and her Uncle Todd saw the girls carrying Miss Kotter, they whisked her off to the nearest hospital. Later they returned to report that her ankle was not broken. The doctor said she would just need to stay off it for a few days.

After Petie opened his presents, everyone helped clean up the park site. Then they headed back home.

Meanwhile, LaToya had devised a plan. (It was a very resourceful plan!) When she shared it with the other PTs, they immediately agreed to it.

That's why the next morning their Sunday school class did have a teacher after all. And they did learn about Moses' sister Miriam and how resourceful she was. They even wrote an "R" for "resourceful" on their Secret Birthday Circles, just as Miss Kotter told them.

By phone, that is. The girls asked Pastor McConahan to plug a telephone in their classroom. Then he turned it to "conference call" so they could all talk and hear Miss Kotter. "This way, Miss Kotter,"

LaToya teased their teacher, "you can be 'hear' without being 'here.' "

Miss Kotter sat at home in her recliner, with her ankle propped up. "That," she told the girls, "is about as resourceful as it comes!"

· Good News · From God's Word

As you read this Bible story, think about what Miriam did or said that was creative or resourceful.

Miriam's Suggestion to a Princess

FROM EXODUS 2:1-10

Miriam's mother could hardly stop crying. Three-year-old Aaron and his big sister Miriam were crying, too. But their baby brother just laughed and gurgled. He was too young to know his life was in grave danger.

The wicked Pharaoh of Egypt had made a rule that all baby boys must die. Miriam's parents loved their children, including their new baby boy. They loved God, too, and knew that killing was wrong. So for three months they hid the baby and tried to keep him quiet. But finally he was too big to hide.

Praying for guidance, his mother made a little basket with a lid. She filled the holes in the basket with tar to make it watertight, and placed a blanket inside. Then she laid her baby in the basket and rocked him. When he was sound asleep, she loosely closed the lid so he wouldn't wake up right away.

Then Miriam and her mother took the basket to the side of the Nile River. There were a lot of tall water plants by the shore. Miriam and her mother hoped someone would see the baby and take pity on him.

Although her mother had to return home, Miriam stayed to watch over the baby basket. She hid and prayed. Soon, one of Pharaoh's daughters, who was a princess, came to the river with her maidens to bathe in the cool waters. When the princess saw the basket and opened it, the baby began crying. "Oh, poor little baby!" she murmured. She took pity on him, just as Miriam and her mother had hoped.

Then Miriam did something very smart and very brave. She approached the princess. "Your Royal Highness," she asked, "would you like for me to find a babysitter for your new baby?"

"Why, yes, thank you!" the princess answered.

So who do you think Miriam suggested? That's right: her own mother! "I'll pay you well to take care of my new baby," the princess told Miriam's mom.

Miriam's whole family was not only safe, they also had more money. Later, the baby grew up to be Moses, the leader of all God's people. But it was his sister Miriam's resourcefulness that helped God's plan to be set in place.

A Verse to Remember

My help comes from the Lord.

— ***Psalm 121:2***

What About You?

Being resourceful means using your mind to think up new and different ways of doing things. For instance, if you hear that your local rescue mission or homeless shelter needs money for their Thanksgiving dinner, you could:

1. Sigh and complain that you're broke.
2. Pester your parents to give money.
3. Try to earn the money yourself by babysitting, raking leaves, washing windows or cars, baking and selling cupcakes, and so on.

If you choose option 3, you are being resourceful.

How can you help someone? Write your idea in the Good Deeds Diary you started on page 72.

When You Need Help

When you have problems, you need answers. Here is a secret for getting help the way Miriam did. Use the code to help you figure out the words below and on the next page. Write each letter on the line beneath its code. Check your answer on page 201.

Secret Code

1 = A	4 = D	5 = E	6 = F	7 = G
8 = H	9 = I	! = K	* = L	& = M
^ = N	% = O	$ = P	@ = R	< = S
> = T	+ = U	(= W	; = Y	

(8 5 ^   ; % +

1 @ 5

< > + & $ 5 4

% ^   (8 1 >

continued on next page…

> % 4 %

_____ _____ _____ _____,

1 < ! 7 % 4

_____ _____ _____ _____ _____ _____

6 % @ 8 5 * $

_____ _____ _____ _____ _____ _____ _____.

8 5 (9 * *

_____ _____ _____ _____ _____ _____

< 5 5 ; % +

_____ _____ _____ _____ _____ _____

> 8 @ % + 7 8

_____ _____ _____ _____ _____ _____ _____!

Secret Letter

Add an "R" for "resourceful" to space 12 of your Secret Birthday Circle on page 44.

Chapter 8

Dunkin' and Punkin'

When the PTs entered their Zone 56 meeting room that Sunday evening, the chalkboard read: "Party Ideas Needed Now!"

"Put on your thinking caps," said Pastor Andy. "because we need to come up with a great party idea."

Pastor Andy continued, "By now most of you have made new friends in your classes this year at school. So we want a fun event for this fall that your new friends would enjoy attending. But also one that honors God."

"What about a game night with a harvest theme?" Sam suggested. "You know, country-style, with 'punkins' and stuff. We can wear jeans and straw hats and big red bandannas."

Josh grinned. "That means LaToya can play her guitar. And Le plays a violin, so she can do some fiddling for us."

"Yee-haw!" Le laughed.

"What about all of the food?" Ryan, another Zone 56 guy, asked. "How much is in our party fund?"

The Zone 56 treasurer, Danielle, checked the balance. With a long face, she said, "Exactly $5.28."

Everyone groaned again, but this time they meant it. "All we can buy with that," Sara sighed, "are the free pumpkins in Kevin's garden. So what do we do now?"

"Why not have a fund-raiser?" Maria asked. "Where I lived before, we used to have car washes. Or we baby-sat. Or helped people put up their storm windows for winter."

"And we could have a kid walking service for trick-or-treat," Sara suggested. "You know, walk kids around their neighborhoods for their parents so they'll be safe. Or take care of babies for parents working at the church Harvest Festival."

Pastor Andy wrote all of the ideas on the chalkboard. "If we set our party date for the first Saturday in November, we'll have time to do all of these things. But it's going to take commitment. You all have ball games, homework and other responsibilities which are all very important. But reaching friends for the Lord is important, too. So if we take on this project, we'll need to consider it a ministry for the Lord. OK?"

The group cheered. "Then let's get on with it!" exclaimed Pastor Andy.

By the end of the meeting, everyone was excited about their upcoming "Punkin' Party," as they decided to call it. And what a party they planned! Lots of pumpkins and cornstalks. Dunking for apples and a whole slew of other fun fall games. Songs, impersonations, jokes. Cider, doughnuts, fried chicken, baked beans. And more!

Le and LaToya made and hung posters all over town. Kevin and Ryan helped them. Sam and Sara handed out fliers at school and to parents at church. Pastor McConahan announced their fund-raisers and party during the worship service. Before long, a lot of Madison kids had agreed to come.

But the morning of the car wash, everyone woke to the steady beat of rain. "Oh, no!" Sam cried as she peered out her bedroom window. "There goes that!"

Much to the kids' surprise, however, when they arrived at the car wash site there were six cars already waiting in line! Even the local newspaper sent a reporter over to snap pictures of them "washing cars in a rainstorm." Then the rain gave way to sunshine and business really picked up. Sam scrubbed until she couldn't move her arms. By the time the Zone 56 members dried the last car, it was dark outside. But their party fund was $75 richer!

The following week several kids from the youth group (and their parents) hung storm windows in return for donations. They stopped by Mrs. Greenleaf's and installed hers for free.

On Halloween, Maria, Sara and Le walked neighborhood children door-to-door to a few homes to get treats. Now that they were too old to trick-or-treat, the PTs realized what fun it was to see the younger children's costumes and talk with the families. After they had visited a few houses, the PTs took the little kids over to Faith Church, where large lights on the church lawn announced the Christian Harvest Festival. Inside, the fellowship hall was alive with music and costumes, plus lots of games, crafts, candy and decorations. The high school youth group staged a play about baby Moses. Pastor McConahan spoke, and all the visiting families received fliers about the church.

LaToya and Sam helped Sam's mom babysit in the church nursery. LaToya was just starting to feed one of the infants when Miss James, the church secretary, rushed in the door.

She looked worried. "LaToya, dear, you have a call in the church office."

LaToya's mother was on the other end of the phone, crying. LaToya's beloved Granny B. had fallen and broken her ankle.

Miss Kotter, now off her own crutches, rushed LaToya to the emergency room to be with her family. Before the night was over, Granny B. was admitted to the hospital. A couple of days later she was released — not to her own home, but to a nursing home: Whispering Pines, the one where Miss Kotter's elderly friend, Ma Jones, lived.

One day after school, Miss Kotter took all the girls to visit Granny B. LaToya brought her guitar along to play for her grandmother.

How glad Granny B. was to see them all! After the nurses propped her up in bed, she sang silly songs with everyone, such as "I've Been Working on the Railroad" and "B-I-N-G-O" and "Bring Back My Bonnie to Me." Then Granny and LaToya sang "Amazing Grace" as a duet.

Patients from up and down the hall started peeking in the doorway and clapping. "More, more!" they called.

Next, the girls went to see Miss Kotter's friend, Ma Jones, and sang for her.

"You've made all the residents so happy today," one of the nurses said. "Could you come back and play for us again sometime? Maybe even help us put on a little party for the residents in our activity room?"

Sam thought about it all the way home. *A party should be for us kids,* the selfish part of her mind said, *not for old people.*

But think how happy you could make them, said her kind, openhearted side.

No! We worked hard to raise all that money! her mean side argued. *We made $250!*

But it was all for Jesus, the kind side argued right back.

Sam's kind side won out. She talked to Miss Kotter about her idea. She also shared it with Pastor Andy, Pastor McConahan, the PTs and the rest of the Zone 56 members. Everyone agreed to move their Punkin' Party to the nursing home and invite all of the residents to attend.

It took some work to let everyone know the change of plans. Anyone who didn't want to go to the nursing home was promised a movie party the next weekend. But only two kids decided not to go. When Mr. Talley, the Madison social studies teacher the PTs disliked, heard about the party, he arranged for a school bus to take everyone there. He was actually turning out to be a very helpful friend!

The Punkin' Party ended up being really fun! No, the residents couldn't participate in all of the games, such as dunking for apples. But the kids chose dunking teams and competed while the patients cheered them on. By the time everything was over, the Zone 56 members were exhausted (and broke!). But they'd never been happier with how a party had turned out.

"I didn't know old people could be such fun," exclaimed one new girl. "We've got to do this again."

Yes, God, Sam prayed. *Thank You for opening all our minds to Your guidance. And our hearts to share Your love. Especially mine!*

· Good News · From God's Word

What if two cents was all the money you had in the world? Just two pennies! Doesn't seem like much, does it? But that's not what Jesus thought! Read on.

A Poor Widow's Offering

FROM LUKE 21:1-4

Did you ever wish you had enough money to do anything in the world? You might dream of fancy houses, fast cars, stylish clothes, far-away trips, big parties or a huge entertainment center. But you probably also tell yourself that you would give away some of your fortune to your church, to poor people or to other good causes like the Salvation Army or the Red Cross. Maybe you dream that your picture would be in the newspaper and on TV, telling everyone how wonderful you are to give away so much. But you'd still have plenty left for all the things you wanted.

That's the way many people felt in Jesus' time on earth. They didn't mind coming to the temple to put a little money in the offering, as long as other people watched them do it. Then others admired them and they felt very good about themselves. Plus they were still very rich!

But one day when Jesus and His friends were at the temple, a very, very poor woman came by. She had no family, no property and no job. Indeed, all the money she had in the world was two little pennies. Maybe she even found them on the street. That's all she had to buy her food or anything else.

But she loved God so much that when she came to His house to worship, she put in an offering: both pennies. Because of her great love for God, the poor woman had faith that He would take care of her if she honored Him.

"She has given more than all the others did!" Jesus said. "For she gave all she had."

A Verse to Remember

God loves a cheerful giver.

— 2 Corinthians 9:7

What About You?

To be "openhearted" means to be like God: open to the hurts and joys and needs of others. An openhearted person doesn't make fun of those who are sick or poor or disabled. She doesn't blame them for their problems. Instead, she reaches out her heart and hands to help them. Here's something to think about:

What if one day when you go to the mall, you find a very old woman sleeping behind a trash bin. She is homeless and you can tell that she has all of her belongings in a shopping cart.

Should you:

1. Scream and run away?
2. Call the police to get rid of her?
3. Get your friends to come and laugh at her or maybe throw things at her?
4. See if your church can find help for her?

If you are openhearted, as God wants you to be, you know that the correct answer is option 4 because you will feel compassion for the woman and want her to be helped.

4J2U

The PTs' church group, Zone 56, has a motto: "4J2U." That stands for "For Jesus to Use." If you are kind and friendly and openhearted, Jesus will use you to show His love to those around you. Find the motto in the puzzle on page 93 by first coloring all the spaces with Xs in them. Then color the rest. (You'll need to flip the page around to read it.) Sam has a sign just like this that she displays like a license plate on her bike! The solution is on page 201.

Secret Letter

Write "O" for "openhearted" in space 11 of your Secret Birthday Circle on page 44.

Chapter 9

Nobody's Nobody

Sara hurried into the Madison gym along with the other students. Seeing her school's head cheerleader, she smiled and waved. "Hi, Brittany!"

Brittany Boorsma was the prettiest and richest girl at Madison Middle School. The most popular, too. She always had a crowd around her.

All fall, Sara had been practicing her cheerleading moves with the hope that she would make Brittany's squad. That's why she tried especially hard to be nice to her. But nothing seemed to work. Ignoring Sara as usual, Brittany breezed right past her with her three closest pals. Brooke, Jennifer and Rachel were all cheerleaders, too. In fact, some kids called them Brittany's "clone club."

That club, of course, didn't include Sara. Sara knew that Jesus said she was to be friendly and kind to everyone. But how could she be friendly to someone who refused to be friendly to her? Brittany wouldn't even speak to her!

Fortunately, Sara had happier things to think about, like the basketball clinic that would begin in just a few minutes. Sam had been on the planning committee. The committee invited some varsity players from Circleville High to help with the demonstrations — including Sara's own brother, Tony!

Sara was so proud of him! Out on the basketball court, his tall, slim, well-muscled frame was the picture of grace and power, especially when he made almost-impossible baskets, one after the other. Sara and Tony looked a lot alike, too, with their freckles and flaming red hair.

Just then, Sam caught Sara's eye. "Save me a seat!" she called. As Sara put her backpack on a seat beside her, Brittany and her "club" moved into the row right in front of her — except for Rachel, who was sitting glumly by herself across the aisle.

Brittany nodded toward Rachel. "What a pain!" she sneered. "All week she's been flirting with Jeremy Pickering. How could she do that when she knows Jeremy's got a thing for me?"

"But, Brittany," Brooke remarked, "what's

wrong with that? You can't even stand the guy."

"So, what's that got to do with it? Any friend of mine who wants to flirt with a guy has to have my permission first. Or they're no friend of mine!"

Just then Coach Pilanto introduced the planning committee and visiting players. A few minutes later, Sam slipped in beside Sara and the demonstrations started.

"Now we all know," the coach began, "that making as many baskets as possible as quickly as possible is the goal of basketball. Today we're privileged to have a super-dunker with us, Circleville High's Tony Fields. Tony's just a sophomore, but he made the varsity team his first season. He has a tremendous point average. At six-feet-one-inch, he's still growing, so this year should be even better. Let's hear it for Tony!"

As everyone cheered, Sam squeezed Sara's hand and grinned. Immediately, Tony started tossing ball after ball without missing a single basket. Brittany squealed. "Oooo! He's cute!"

Sara leaned forward. "Thanks, Brittany. I think my brother's cute, too."

Whirling around, the head cheerleader gave her a dirty look. Then she glanced back at Tony and her mouth flew open. Finally, she stammered, "Well, I didn't know you had a brother, Sara. Shame he got all the looks in your family. But we might just let you on our squad after all. It's for sure me and my pals could do a lot more for you than the nobodies you hang around with now."

Brittany, sneering, nodded toward Sam. "You know, like her."

Sara stared at Brittany, shocked. For months she had longed to be a Madison cheerleader. For months she and her other friends from Faith Church had also been inviting Brittany to their youth group. Brittany always laughed at them. "Church is for wimps," she had said. "For nobodies. Not for winners like me and my friends."

Please, dear Lord, Sara prayed to herself, *give me the words to say back to her.*

Finally, she replied, "I would be glad to be your friend, Brittany. Brooke's and Jennifer's, too. And Rachel's. Sam's, too. And a friend to everyone here. We're all from Madison, so we're all on the same team. 'Go Madison,' right?"

Suddenly, she relaxed. "But Sam and I are on another team, too, Brittany. So is my big brother, Tony, and lots of our friends. The real way to be somebody is through Jesus. 'Cause with Him, nobody's a nobody. Maybe one of these days you can come to church with us and find out what I mean."

Then, as Brittany's mouth flew open with angry astonishment, Sara added with a smile, "And learn more about my good-looking brother, too!"

· Good News · From God's Word

Sara learned the importance of love and loyalty in true friendship — the same lesson that Ruth and Naomi learned long ago.

Ruth's Love and Loyalty

FROM RUTH 1-3

Naomi and her husband once lived in Israel. But when times became hard, they moved to Moab. Their two young sons grew up there. After Naomi's husband died, both young men fell in love with Moabite girls. One son chose to marry Orpah, and the other married Ruth.

Naomi's sons' brides were good to her and helped her. They came to love God just as she did.

Those happy times were over when both sons suddenly died. Naomi cried and cried. "I'm going back to Israel," she sobbed, "to my hometown of Bethlehem. I want you girls to go back to your hometowns, too. Maybe you'll find new husbands to marry."

"No! No!" both young women protested. "We love you too much to leave you."

Finally, Orpah agreed to go back to her own parents. But Ruth insisted that real love between people wasn't just for good days. Love was for days with problems, too. It's loyal and long-lasting. "Please," Ruth begged, "let me go with you and take care of you. Don't let anything but death separate us!"

So Ruth did go to Bethlehem with Naomi. Working together, both of them found happiness there. In fact, in her new home Ruth fell in love and married again. Ruth and her husband included Naomi in their family and took care of her. Ruth later had a baby boy named Obed who became the grandfather of King David!

A Verse to Remember

A friend loves at all times.

— Proverbs 17:17

Friends or Frights?

As you read the questions below and on the next page, ask yourself: Is the person described the kind you'd like to have for your own best friend? Check "yes" or "no" in the first column. Next ask: Is the person described the kind of friend you'd like to be? Check "yes" or "no" in the second column. Compare your answers to those on page 201.

	Want to Have		Want to Be	
1. Is jealous of my other friends.	yes __	no __	yes __	no __
2. Ignores me when others are around.	yes __	no __	yes __	no __
3. Won't let me be alone when I need to be.	yes __	no __	yes __	no __
4. Is kind and helpful and seldom complains.	yes __	no __	yes __	no __
5. Remembers birthdays and special days.	yes __	no __	yes __	no __
6. Tells mean or dirty jokes.	yes __	no __	yes __	no __

continued on next page...

7. Talks about people behind their backs.

yes __ no __ yes __ no __

8. Is polite and nice to my whole family.

yes __ no __ yes __ no __

9. Tells secrets and spreads gossip about people.

yes __ no __ yes __ no __

10. Wants to live a life pleasing to God.

yes __ no __ yes __ no __

If you need help learning how to be a loving, loyal friend, ask Jesus. He's the best friend in the world!

How Sweet It Is!

From the list below, select the best rhyming word to complete each blank in the sentences on the next page. Then copy the poem on a small sheet of paper, including the missing words. Sign it, fold it and slip it into a bag of candy, fruit or other goodies for your best friend.

A. you B. team C. right

D. friend E. do

1. Inside "friend" there is an "end"
2. Yet there's no end to being a ________.

continued on next page…

3. For friends are loyal, friends are true.

4. Helping each other is what friends _________.

5. Friends don't lie or yell or fight.

6. They help each other do what's _________.

7. Though hard the task to do may seem,

8. Friends work together as a _________.

9. Friends help to see each other through.

10. That's why I'm glad for a friend like __________!

Check your answers on page 202.

Secret Letter

Add an "L" for "loyal" to space 10 of your Secret Birthday Circle on page 44.

Chapter 10

Stupid, Nasty Cold!

LaToya had never been busier or happier. She loved playing guitar for the 4J2U Praise Band at church. Now she was playing at school, too, for the jazz choir. In between, she took gymnastics and did a zillion fun things with her just-as-busy PTs.

For her English project, LaToya had to write about someone very special. No one was as special to

LaToya as her Granny B.! So each week, LaToya took her tape recorder to the Whispering Pines Nursing Home to see her grandmother. Afterward, she typed the "interview" on her family's computer.

Each evening, LaToya also started dinner for her family. Her mother, an English teacher at the high school, usually got home late because she often stayed after school to tutor students. Her big sister, Tina, a college nursing student, lived at home to save money. But now that Tina worked part-time at the Midway Mall, she was hardly ever around. Their dad worked nights at the supermarket, so LaToya didn't see him much, either.

But one thing her family did do together that fall was get flu shots. Even Granny B. Just in case.

So LaToya was surprised several days later at school to suddenly feel strange and weak. First she was hot. Then she was freezing cold. Then she starting coughing and couldn't stop.

The school nurse took her temperature. "You have a fever, my dear," Mrs. Ammons said. "We'd better get you home right away."

When LaToya dragged in the front door that afternoon, Tina was just ready to leave for a class. But she took one look at her sister and shook her head. "You're one sick kid," she said. "I'm going to give you some aspirin and something cold to drink. Then you're going right to bed until Mom gets here."

"But I can't be sick," LaToya mumbled. "I got a flu shot."

"Yes, but you didn't got a cold shot. There is

no way to keep from getting colds. Mom's got some chicken soup frozen, so I'll put some out to thaw before I leave. Then Mom can heat it up when she gets home. I'd stay, but I've got to take a midterm in chemistry. I'd almost rather be in bed with a cold!"

"You poor child," Mrs. Thomas sighed when she came home. "A cold, is it? There's a lot of that going around at our school, too. I'll get some soup warmed up for you right away. And some nice, buttered toast with honey. Now don't you worry about trying to do homework tonight. No school for you tomorrow."

"Do I need to go to the doctor?"

"Not for a regular cold. But we'll keep an eye on your temperature. If it gets too high, I'll take you over to the urgent care clinic."

Even though LaToya felt miserable, it was nice to have her mother "baby" her. Stuffy nose, upset stomach, splitting headache. She felt awful everywhere. And she looked it, too, with a red nose, red eyes and a sad, drooping mouth. "Stupid, nasty cold!" she muttered. Her mom looked very tired, too. But she always got up to help LaToya, put something cold on her forehead and gently pat her back.

When LaToya's dad came home from work the next morning, he was dead-tired. But then he found out LaToya was sick. So instead of going to bed, he took care of her while Mrs. Thomas and Tina were gone. At noon, he smiled wearily after taking her temperature. "Your fever's down some, gal. You're going to make it. Now I'm going to get some sleep."

The next day, Sam and Maria brought LaToya a new puzzle to give her something to do while she was sick. Miss Kotter stopped by with flowers and a funny card. Pastor Andy called to see how she was doing. "Awful," she croaked pitifully. But actually, she was already starting to feel a little better. And her temperature was now normal.

That weekend, Whispering Pines called. Granny B.'s ankle had healed and she was ready to come home.

Everyone was so thrilled to see her! When LaToya's dad pushed her wheelchair into the living room, they all cheered. Mrs. Thomas got Granny B.'s bed ready for her, cooked her favorite food and hugged her over and over.

But wait a minute, LaToya thought. *Why is everyone making such a big fuss over Granny B. when I am still sick? That's not fair! Why doesn't someone make a fuss over me?* LaToya went back to her room to pout.

She looked at the beautiful flowers Miss Kotter had brought her, and then thought of the Bible story from the week before about a wealthy woman who was always looking for ways to help others. That's why she built Elisha his own place to stay. "She was a kind, thoughtful woman," Miss Kotter had said. "Remember, 'T' is for 'thoughtful.' "

The next morning, LaToya still felt weak and shaky. But as soon as she jumped out of bed and washed her face, she felt a lot better. She hurried to Granny B.'s room. "We're so glad to have you home, Granny B.!" she said, and meant it. "What would you like this morning? Hot coffee? Bacon? Oatmeal? Fruit and cereal?"

Her grandmother still looked pale and tired. But she opened her arms. "I've been needing me a hug, little girl. One about a million miles wide!"

LaToya was happy to give her the biggest one she could muster.

· Good News · From God's Word

While you read the following Bible story, be thinking of something you can do to help someone else.

A Kind Hostess Helping Elisha

FROM 2 KINGS 4:8-11

Back in the prophet Elisha's day, God's people didn't have a lot of churches. There weren't many pastors to tell people about God's Word. So Elisha traveled around the land, helping people learn the right way to live.

One day he came to the town of Shunem. A wealthy woman there was very glad to see him.

"Please come and have dinner with my husband and me," she said. When he agreed, she prepared him a wonderful meal. Elisha enjoyed talking with her and her husband about the things of the Lord. When he was ready to leave, she said, "Stop back here next time you're in town. OK?"

Soon Elisha was coming there often. The wealthy couple were always glad to welcome him for a meal. But the prophet really needed a place to stay when he traveled there — a private place to sleep and pray. So the woman said to her husband, "Why don't we build an upstairs addition on our house, big enough for an outside staircase and a room? With the outside door, he can go in and out whenever he wants."

By the next time Elisha came to Shunem, the room was all ready. Elisha must have been thankful for this kind, thoughtful woman and her husband!

A Verse to Remember

Look not only to your own interests,
but also to the interests of others.

— Philippians 2:4

What About You?

Sometimes we think we have to do something big to impress someone, or not even try. But that's not so. Think how glad your family would be if you offered on your own to do the dishes one night or walk the dog or clean out the car. How about babysitting your younger sister or brother? Could you learn to make spaghetti or tacos for the family? You know you could water your mom's indoor plants for her. At the very least, you could offer to rub your dad's back when he is tired.

As Sara said to Brittany at the basketball demonstration, "We're all on the same team." A thoughtful girl like you can make a great team member for your family!

Secret Letter

Add a "T" for "thoughtful" to space 1 of your Secret Birthday Circle on page 44.

Happy Searching!

Ways to show your thoughtfulness are listed below. The suggestions are also hidden inside the word search on the next page. See how many you can find. Remember, words can go up, down, across, backward or diagonally. You might enjoy doing this word search with a friend. Then the two of you can plan to do a "thoughtful good deed" together! The answer key is on page 202.

Word List

babysit
bake a cake
build
clean bird cage
clean room
clean sidewalk
do dishes
dust
edge yard
feed cat
give massage
help with dinner
iron
knit
mend
mow lawn
paint
polish
rake leaves
scrub shower
set table
sew
shop
shovel snow
sweep
vacuum
walk dog
wash car
wash dog
wash windows
weed

D O D I S H E S E T T A B L E

U X X M D E E W X X G C X X X

S R D O P L X E E S I L S X X

T A L O O P X E D C V E W C W

M C I R L W K P G R E A O L O

O H U N I I N X E U M N D E N

W S B A S T I S Y B A B N A S

L A V E H H T X A S S I I N L

A W A L K D O G R H S R W S E

W A C C T I X X D O A D H I V

N S U P N N X X X W G C S D O

I H U O I N X X X E E A A E H

R D M H A E W E S R X G W W S

O O X S P R E K A C A E K A B

N G R A K E L E A V E S X L X

X X M E N D T A C D E E F K X

Chapter 11

A Bear of a Science Fair

Sam's hand shot up in the air. Mrs. Eldridge, her science teacher, nodded. "Yes, Sam?"

"Did you say we can use any subject we want for our science fair project this year?"

"Any subject that's in good taste. The emphasis is on honest research, study and testing. You should use good scientific methods to discover things about your subject, which won't necessarily be what you thought you'd discover."

She continued, "Now I want everyone to pick a team partner. If you can't find one, I'll match you up. Together, pick a subject. By tomorrow at the latest, hand me in written form the name of your subject and how you plan to study it."

Maria and Le paired off. So did Sara and LaToya. Sam chose Jenna Jenkins, who was new to Madison this year. She was tall and willowy and wore a ponytail high on her head, like a dancer's crown. Jenna went to the Zone 56 Punkin' Party at Whispering Pines. She said she had a good time. But she hadn't been back to church since.

"Hey, Le," Maria began, "do you like bugs?"

"Bugs? You mean the kind in computers?"

Maria giggled. "No, silly. The creepy-crawly kind. What if we study the insects in one little section outside the school? We could keep a record of the types and take pictures of them. Maybe we could even bring some in for display. It would be neat to see how many disappear when it snows and how many of them find places to hide.

Le smiled. "Sure. As long as you're the one to touch them, not me. Yuck!"

Sara and LaToya decided to do a study on sunflower seeds as a food, and how many ways sunflower seeds could be prepared or used.

Jenna looked discouraged. "I've never even been to a science fair before," she sighed. "I don't even know where to begin with ideas."

Sam's eyes twinkled. "I do. With bears!"

"You mean the big, scary kind?

"No, soft, cuddly ones! Like those on my bed."

Jenna smiled. "I have some, too!"

Both girls happened to have huge collections of bears sprawling across their beds and shelves and falling out of their closets. Pink bears, blue ones, huge ones, tiny ones, plush ones, ceramic ones — they had them all!

"We'll see which kinds people prefer," Sam said. "Maybe we can hold a bear fair at the library. You know, display our bear collection and lots of books about bears. Maybe the librarian could read bear stories to the little kids. What do you think?"

Jenna giggled. "I think it's a beary good idea! But what does it have to do with science? I thought we were supposed to cut up frogs or something."

"We'll make theories about what kind of people would prefer which kind — you know, boys, girls, babies, old people. Then we'll ask everyone who comes to our bear fair which kind they really do like and why. Then we can do all the statistics and make a big report and chart."

Jenna wrinkled her nose. "Well, I hate math. But I love bears. Let's do it!"

The bear fair was a huge success. In fact,

Jenna's calculator could hardly keep up with all the numbers. They found that of the 233 people who passed by the display, 180 stopped. About a third were kids their age, a third were younger children and a third were adults. Most people preferred the old-fashioned, large brown "teddy" bears. Almost 25 children checked out bear books after studying the exhibit. Nearly all of the viewers filled out the bear fair scoring sheet that Sam and Jenna provided. Jenna's mom came by and took lots of pictures.

"This is great!" Sam said exuberantly as they bagged up their bears to leave. "I bet Mrs. Eldridge will be thrilled with our project."

Sara and LaToya were also doing well with their idea. They researched the different ways sunflower seeds could be prepared, both for snacks and for cooking. They also set up a sunflower tray for birds and noted which feathered friends liked which kind. Not only did they copy down sunflower seed recipes, they got the school cafeteria to start using them in breads and salads.

As for Le and Maria, they checked their "insect ranch" each day. Then they entered the statistics in Le's computer and printed them out. They found a lot of information in the library and on the Internet, including the bugs' long, scientific names.

Other kids used computers in their projects, too. They studied space, rockets, video games, history, sports, finances and endangered animals. So when they heard about Sam and Jenna's bear project, they teased, "Don't you know this is middle school, not preschool?"

The girls smiled back. "You just can't *bear* to see us win!" Sam said.

That night as Sam and Jenna designed their science fair display board, Sam sighed. "I wish we could make our report more interesting instead of writing the dull, old truth. Making stuff up is more fun, isn't it?"

Jenna looked at her strangely. "Is that what you want to do?"

"No, it's what I'm tempted to do. But I know it wouldn't be right. It wouldn't be responsible and honest. It's not the 4J2U way. So I wouldn't do it."

"For Jay who?'"

Laughing, Sam explained that "4J2U" stood for "For Jesus to Use." "It's not always easy to do the right thing. But when I ask God to help me, He always does it."

Jenna smiled. "I'm glad you feel that way, Sam. I do, too."

The whole school was invited to the science fair, including parents. Miss Kotter came by on her lunch hour. Maria's and Le's "Watch Where You Step" project about insects tied for first place with an experiment on drinking water. LaToya and Sara tied for second place with their "Let's All Go to Seed!"

which featured their sunflower sunshine cookies.

But Sam's and Jenna's "Get Your Hugs Here" was the favorite of all the younger children. "You know, Sam," Jenna said when they finally took down their display, "it's been fun working with you. I think maybe I need more 4J2U in my life, too! Can you help me find it?"

· Good News · from God's Word

God helped Sam be responsible and do what's right, even when she was tempted to do something else. Here is a Bible story about another girl God helped to do the right thing.

Abishag's Care of King David

FROM 1 KINGS 1:1-4

"King David is ill!"

Messengers rushed through Israel with the sad news. Their elderly king was so sick that he shook violently with chills. No matter how many royal robes and blankets they put on him, his friends and servants couldn't keep David warm.

"He needs a full-time nurse," they finally decided. "A young woman with the strength to take care of him day and night." So they sent their messengers to find one.

Of course, all the young women in the country wanted to help. They all loved King David. They loved the psalms and songs that he wrote. But not many young women in Israel were trained for nursing. They didn't know how to help someone who was gravely ill.

Then the king's messengers found Abishag. She was not only beautiful, she was kind and hard-working, too. She knew how to provide all the care the sick king needed.

Abishag left her home to go live in a fancy palace. It might have been fun for Abishag to meet important people and go to parties while she lived in the palace — a lot more fun than taking care of a very sick patient! But Abishag was responsible. She could be trusted to do what was right. Day and night, she stayed at King David's side until he began to feel better. Abishag was given a special job. She worked hard to fulfill her duties.

A Verse to Remember

Whatever you do, work at it with all your heart, as working for the Lord.

— Colossians 3:23

What About You?

Describe your first doll:

____

____

____

Describe your favorite doll:

____

____

____

Describe your first stuffed animal:

____

____

____

Do you collect any stuffed animals now? ___________

If you have a collection, write about it here:

____

____

____

To Be or Not to Be

To discover a new bear friend, color in all the spaces in the puzzle on the next page that don't have B's in them. Then color the bear. See the finished puzzle on page 202.

Secret Letter

Add an "R" for "responsible" to space 3 of your Secret Birthday Circle on page 44.

Chapter 12

I Hate to Skate!

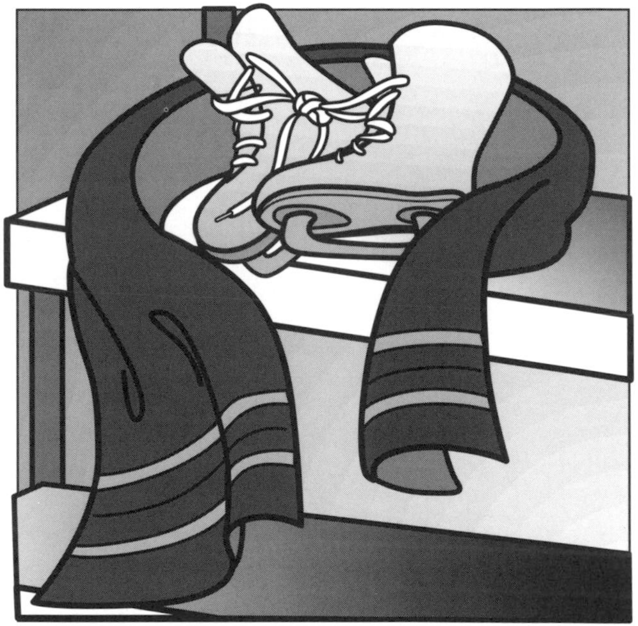

The following Sunday, the PTs studied about Mary and Martha, who served Jesus.

"Remember," Miss Kotter said, "they didn't just serve Him because they had to or because of good manners or doing their duty. They did it out of love — the way all of us should serve God, and others, too. So your secret letter this week is 'E' for 'eager to serve.' "

After the lesson, Sara asked, "Miss Kotter, do you like to ice skate?"

Their teacher laughed. "I used to, but I haven't skated for years. Why?"

"Well, I was just thinking. Maybe we could all go skating one night this week. Our families, too, if they want. To help us get in the mood for Christmas!"

"Christmas? It's not even Thanksgiving yet!"

Sam joined in. "Please? It would be so much fun."

"OK, if you're all for it. What about Friday night? Check with your parents and call me."

That Friday evening, a snowflake fell on Sam's nose as she waited outside the Ice Palace. Beside her, Petie and Suzie wiggled and giggled with excitement. Soon the whole gang arrived, including Maria's twin brothers, Juan and Ricardo, and her little sister, Lolita. Everyone's breath made white puffs in the frosty, clear air.

Inside, as they laced on their skates, Sam's mom said excitedly. "I don't think I've done this in at least 10 years!"

"I'm glad we've got adults along to help babysit," Sara whispered to Sam. "I want to try some new moves all by myself. I used to take skating lessons — I hope I haven't forgotten everything."

Sam looked around at the crowded rink. "We won't be able to do much without running into each other. But we can have fun anyway. Look! Le's already doing twirls! Hey, I see some of the guys from church. Maybe we can get a game going with them."

On her second time around the ice, Sam glanced at the spectators' benches. LaToya's Granny B. waved to her. Granny B.'s wheelchair was covered with a gigantic blanket, just like the gigantic smile on her face. LaToya was glad to see her feeling well again.

But she wasn't alone. Miss Kotter was with her. So were Mrs. Pearson, Mrs. Fields and Maria. And so were Petie, Juan, Ricardo, Lolita and Suzie! They all had their skates on, but nobody was skating. What in the world was wrong?

Sam stopped. "Hey, you guys, the ice is great! Come on out!"

"No, it's not!" Petie sobbed. "I hate the ice! It won't even let me stand up!"

"We have a problem, Sam," Miss Kotter explained. "None of the little kids know how to skate. Maria doesn't, either. Do you think you girls could help us out with a little training class? That way everyone can have fun tonight."

No! It's not fair! Sam stormed to herself. *I don't want to babysit! I want to have fun with my friends!*

Then she looked at the sad children and felt ashamed of herself. "Well, sure. I'll go get the other girls. And the guys, too. We should have everyone skating in no time. Or at least able to stand up!"

Soon, with a helper on each side, and one in back as well, each skater-to-be was helped out on the ice. A cheer went up for each step, each slide, each glide. And laughter for each crash. But after a while each of the learners could yell, "Hey, Granny B.! Did you see me skate? I really, really skated!"

Other kids rushed over to Sam and her friends. "Could you teach us, too? Please?"

They even asked Maria. She laughed. "I'm just learning myself! But I can teach you what I know."

Later during a break from the ice, as Sam poured Granny B. a mug of hot chocolate, Granny B. said, "I'm proud of you girls. You made a lot of children happy tonight by being so eager to serve. Now I'll tell the little ones a story while you older ones have fun by yourselves." Then she turned to Miss Kotter, "You grown-ups, too. Shoo!"

They had a ball! Sam's and Sara's moms and Miss Kotter put their arms around each other's waists and skated together. Sara found she could skate almost as fast as Ryan Nelson, one of the Zone 56 guys. "When I get to high school I'm going to try out for the ice hockey team," he told her.

"Well, guess what?" she teased. "Maybe I'll be team captain!"

Sam was glad that God had helped all of them to be eager to serve Him. And to serve others, too.

· Good News · from God's Word

Sometimes we think only adult pastors and missionaries serve God. Read on to find out how Mary and Martha learned to serve God right in their home!

Mary and Martha Serving Jesus

FROM LUKE 10:38-42

"Oh, Jesus!" Martha cried when she saw her beloved friend. "I'm so glad you're in town. You must come to our house for dinner today. I won't take no for an answer."

"Please, Jesus!" her sister Mary echoed. "I have so many things I want to talk to you about!"

Martha was a very good cook. She loved to please her guests with wonderful meals. Especially

Jesus. He had brought so much happiness and joy and hope into her life. Nothing was too good for her friend and Savior. So she cooked and cooked and cooked and cooked! Even when Jesus finally got to her house, Martha was too busy cooking and cleaning to spend time with Him.

Mary helped with the cooking, too. But she couldn't bear not to be with Jesus. So every few minutes, she rushed in and sat at His feet to listen to Him explain God's Word.

Martha didn't like that. She stormed into the sitting room. "Lord, look at my lazy sister! She just sits there while I have to do all the work. Make her come help me."

Jesus smiled. He knew that both women loved Him and were eager to serve Him.

"Martha, Martha," He said, "you are worried about many things. But, believe it or not, learning about God is more important than cooking the finest meal in the world."

A Verse to Remember

Serve one another in love.

— Galatians 5:13

What About You?

Serving others doesn't mean being a slave or a "door mat." In the situations below, pick the one that best describes a sensible, loving, helpful way to honor God. Check your answers on page 202.

1. Your little sister needs help with her homework. But you need to take a shower and pack a lunch for school the next day. So you:

a. tell your sister you can't help her.

b. help your sister and go dirty and hungry to school the next day.

c. take a shower, then talk through your sister's homework with her while you pack your lunch.

2. Your mom wants you to wash the dishes after dinner. You want to talk on the phone to your best friend. So you:

a. yell, "Why can't we get a dishwasher like everyone else?"

b. hurry and do the dishes so you can talk all you want.

c. do the dishes, grumbling the whole time.

3. Your teacher asks you to help clean the chalkboards. You'd rather talk to Mary about her party. So you:

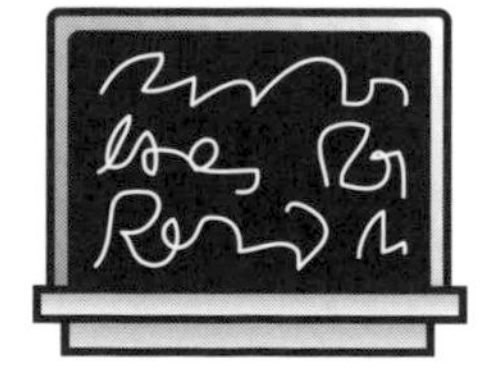

a. ask if Mary can clean them with you.

b. pretend you have to leave early, so you can't help your teacher.

c. clean the boards, but not be very happy about it.

Doing Figure 8's

In the coded message below and on the next page, first cross through all the 8's. Then use the Secret Code to fill in the letters of all the words. Write the letters on the lines and learn a great way to develop a "gratitude attitude."

Secret Code

* = A	% = C	$ = D	¨ = E	≠ = F
& = G	Æ = H	Ø = I	© = L	ø = M
∫ = N	x = O	π = P	√ = R	Δ = S
# = T	[= V	] = W	? = Y	

Δ 8 ¨ 8 √ [¨   & 8 x $ 8

______________   ______________

¨ 8 * & 8 ¨ 8 √ © ?   8] Ø 8 # Æ

______________   ______________

© 8 x 8 [¨   * 8 ∫ 8 $

______________   ______________

continued on next page…

& 8 √ 8 * 8 % ¨   8 *

Æ 8 ¨ 8 © 8 π Ø 8 ∫ &   Æ 8 * ∫ 8 $

* 8 ∫ 8 $ * 8

Δ 8 ø Ø 8 © Ø 8 ∫ &   8 ≠ * 8 % 8 ¨

Check your answers on page 203.

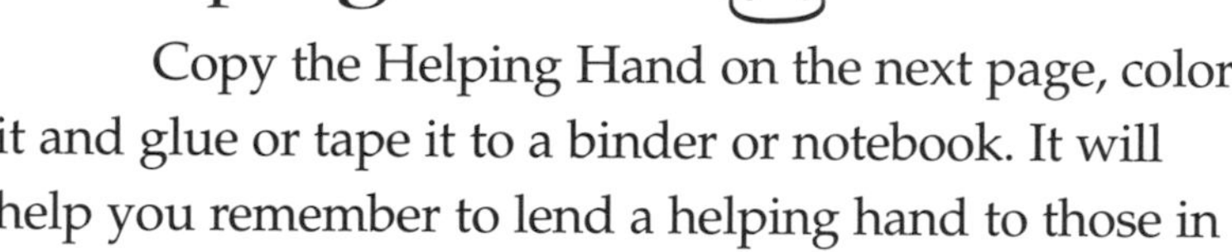

A Helping Hand

Copy the Helping Hand on the next page, color it and glue or tape it to a binder or notebook. It will help you remember to lend a helping hand to those in need — and to do it with a smile!

Secret Letter

Add an "E" for "eager to serve" in space 9 of your Secret Birthday Circle on page 44.

Chapter 13

Company's Coming!

When Maria arrived home from school, her mom had exciting news.

"Your Aunt Luz just called. Your Uncle Marcel is coming to Danville on business the Monday after Thanksgiving."

"Wow! That's not far from Circleville. I hope we get to see him, Mama."

"Actually, we'll not only get to see him. Your Aunt Luz and the kids are driving up with him! They'll come for Thanksgiving and stay with us for the whole weekend. Won't it be fun to have them visit in our new house?"

Maria hugged her mother. "That's great, Mama! I'll tell Le about it when I go see her in a few minutes. We're going to work on our science project together."

Mrs. Moreno was already preparing dinner. "Ah, that gives me an idea. Why don't you invite her and her dear mother to join us for Thanksgiving, too? The more the merrier, *si*?"

She continued, "If we don't have room for everyone to eat in the dining room, we'll use the rec room in the basement or set up card tables or something. Getting a little messy is not as important as showing a lot of love, *si*? Be sure to bundle up before you go out. This drizzle is supposed to turn to rain very soon. Maybe even snow."

"*Si*, Mama. I've got my umbrella. And I'll be back in time to set the table."

Le had her computer up and running when Maria arrived. "Stick with your studying, girls," her mother warned from the next room. "No video games."

Then Mrs. Tran came into Le's room. Maria's mouth flew open. "Oh, Mrs. Tran! You look beautiful!"

And she did. Already dressed for that evening's concert, she wore a long, white satin gown embroidered with graceful birds and blossoms. Her floor-length black cape was lined with shimmering red satin. Le smiled proudly at her mother.

Then Maria remembered her own mother's invitation. "Mrs. Tran, if you and Le don't have plans for Thanksgiving, we'd love to have you eat with us. 'The more the merrier,' Mama says!"

"Maybe we can all go together to the Thanksgiving Eve services at church, too," Le added.

Maria grinned. "Ooo! That would be great."

"Tell your mother thank you," Mrs. Tran replied. She didn't say "yes," but she didn't say "no" either.

After Le's mom left, the girls started on their assignment. Mrs. Eldridge, their science teacher, had been very pleased with their science fair project on insects. "There will be a county science fair later this year," she had informed them. "I'd like for you girls to enter it. Expand your research. Add more places to check for insects, like inside the school, around your homes, by Lucky Lake or on a sidewalk."

So earlier that day, Le and Maria had looked for insects throughout their school building. Now as Le typed their research on the computer, Maria suggested, "Maybe we should change our project's name to 'Help! We're Being Bugged!' " They both laughed.

By the time Maria headed home, light rain had changed to huge snowflakes. When she walked in her own front door, cold and hungry, she smelled steaming, hot enchiladas.

When she finally took her last bite, Maria asked, "Where's our company going to sleep, Mama?"

"Well, I've been thinking about that. We have the three bedrooms, plus the living room sofa bed and the couch in the basement. Also, our old foldaway cot. Your aunt and uncle can have the master bedroom. Jamie's 5, so he can be in with Juan and Ricardo. The other three boys can be in your and Lolita's room. Your papa and I will use the sofa bed, with a cot nearby for Lolita. Or she could sleep down in the basement with you. What do you think?"

Maria's mouth flew open. Sleep in the basement? Suddenly she wanted to cry. Why couldn't her stupid cousins sleep in the basement instead of her? It wasn't fair!

The next day at school, Le said, "Oh, Maria! It's so great that you've invited us for Thanksgiving. Mom's so excited. She's already planning a big dessert to bring over and share. It's so great to have unselfish friends like you."

But Maria didn't feel very unselfish. She was still seething over having to give up her room to guests. *Can't you change my mom's mind, Lord?* she prayed silently.

That Sunday, the PTs' Sunday school lesson was about a very poor widow who was willing to give up the last food she had to help a starving minister. "I could give up my food, too," Maria said to herself. "But not my own bed. Not my own bedroom. Yet I do love my cousins. Why is this so hard?"

On Tuesday, Sam invited all the PTs to her house to make pumpkin bread and popcorn. But even with all the fun, Maria still felt miserable inside.

The next evening, it took two cars to transport everyone in Maria's family, their guests, Le and her mom to the Thanksgiving Eve service. Huge, white flakes floated down from the sky and plopped on the windshield. It was like being in a real-life Christmas card!

Pastor McConahan talked about how everyone should be grateful for the blessings God had given them: food, families, health, warm clothes and a bed to sleep in.

"All these we are thankful for. But God's Word also says that a 'gratitude attitude' includes helping others who don't have those blessings," he said. "We need to do all we can to help them be warm, dry, healthy and filled, too. That's why we're taking up a special offering tonight for the Circleville Rescue Mission."

Just then Le heard something strange. It was Maria! She was sobbing. *Sweet Maria,* Le thought, *she's feeling sorry for those poor people at the mission.*

After the service, Maria confessed to Le that she had actually been feeling sorry for herself. "I was so mad about sleeping in the basement. Then during the service I began thinking about all those homeless people with no place at all to sleep. And how wonderful it was that Uncle Marcel's family could come. And what a wonderful Thanksgiving we're all going to have.

"Then I realized I was just being selfish. And I was so ashamed of myself, I started crying and asked God to forgive me."

Le gave Maria a warm hug. "Hey, I'd love to have you stay at my house tonight! We have lots of room. Your little sister can come, too. Ooo… three girls! That would be like having sisters of my very own. Our own slumber party! Let's ask our moms about it."

That night, after the excited girls finally quieted down with Maria and Lolita snuggled up in Le's spare bunk bed, Maria prayed to herself: *Please, dear Lord, forgive me for being so selfish. Help me have an unselfish 'gratitude attitude' toward others. And thank You for my wonderful family and friends. In Jesus' name. Amen.*

· Good News · from God's Word

It's easy to share when you have plenty of something. But what if someone asks you to share all that you have? Read on.

A Widow Shares with Elijah

from 1 Kings 17:7-16

Wearing threadbare clothes, the young mother walked slowly around the fields outside her city's gate. Now and then she leaned over to pick up a piece of dry wood. After months of famine, firewood was all that was left in the fields. Many people had died of starvation, including her own husband. She and her little boy would probably die next.

Just then a stranger came up to the gate. The prophet Elijah had walked a long way. "My good woman," he called to her, "could you please bring me a little water to drink?"

"Why, yes, of course," she replied. Then as she started back to her house to get a drink for him, he added, "And a little piece of bread, too, please."

Tears sprang to her eyes. "Oh, sir, as surely as God lives, there's not even a crumb in my house. Just a tiny bit of flour in a jar and a tiny bit of oil in a jug. That's why I'm gathering this firewood — to cook one last little meal. After that, my son and I will have to starve to death."

Then Elijah told her something amazing: "If you use that tiny bit of flour to make some bread for me, there will be enough left over to make more for you and your little boy. In fact, you will never run out of food again!"

God helped the woman believe, and Elijah's word indeed came true. God took care of her because she gave so unselfishly to His prophet.

A Verse to Remember

What I have I give you.

— ***Acts 3:6***

What About You?

There are people in need in every city, town or rural area. Many are sick, out of work or homeless. Some people can't see or hear or walk well enough to take care of themselves. They may be young or old, or victims of terrible disasters like floods, tornadoes, fires, hurricanes or earthquakes.

Find out what problems affect people in your own area and what's being done to help them. Look around, read the newspaper and ask others. (But don't wander anywhere dangerous by yourself.) Write your discoveries on the next page.

Problems in my area:

____

____

____

____

What I can do to help:

____

____

____

____

Maybe your friends or your church can take up a sharing and caring offering for a much-needed ministry.

Secret Letter

Add a "U" for "unselfish" in space 2 of your Secret Birthday Circle on page 44.

Quick Pumpkin Bread

Here's how to make pumpkin bread like the PTs baked at Sam's house. Be sure an adult is nearby for safety when using the oven.

What You Need

- 9" x 5" loaf pan
- non-stick cooking spray
- large bowl
- measuring cups and spoons
- large spoon
- 1¾ cups sifted, all-purpose flour
- ¼ teaspoon baking powder
- 1 teaspoon baking soda
- 1 teaspoon salt
- ½ teaspoon cinnamon
- ¼ teaspoon ground cloves
- 1⅓ cups sugar
- ⅓ cup shortening
- 2 eggs
- 1 cup canned pumpkin
- ⅓ cup water or milk
- ½ teaspoon vanilla
- ½ cup chopped nuts
- ⅓ cup raisins

What to Do

1. Preheat the oven to 350 degrees.

2. Spray the pan with non-stick cooking spray.

3. Sift together the flour, baking powder, baking soda, salt, cinnamon and ground cloves. Set aside.

4. In a large bowl, beat together the sugar, shortening and eggs.

5. Add and beat in the pumpkin.

6. Add the dry ingredients in slowly, along with the water or milk and the vanilla.

7. Fold (stir) in the nuts and the raisins.

8. Pour the batter into a greased pan and bake about 1 hour. Allow to cool before slicing.

Chapter 14

The Nuttiest Thanksgiving Ever!

Sam was glad Maria and Le would be having such a great time at Maria's on Thanksgiving.

Every year, Sam's relatives got together, too. Uncle Todd, Aunt Caitlin and Suzie all lived in Circleville, of course. But Grandma and Grandpa Pearson, Uncle Dwayne and Aunt Irene and their sons lived in Michigan.

"Dwayne's boys are all big teenagers," Mr. Pearson said. "If I remember right, they can eat us out of house and home. So we'd better get a big turkey *and* a whole lot of hamburgers!"

"Yes," Mrs. Pearson agreed. "Dwayne's family and your mom and dad will be in from Detroit on Wednesday and are going to stay right through the weekend, so it will be impossible to have too much food on hand!"

On Saturday when Sam and her mom went grocery shopping, their list was practically a mile long. Grocery bags filled the entire van!

On Sunday morning, Sam gave Miss Kotter a hug. " I wish you could be with us on Thanksgiving, too," Sam told her.

"That's sweet of you," her teacher replied. "Maria's family also invited me. But I'm spending the day helping at the Circleville Rescue Mission. Homeless people need a little Thanksgiving joy in their lives, too, and I know the mission needs as many volunteers as they can get on Thanksgiving."

That week, Sam's house was a flurry of preparations. Within days, cakes, pies, candied apples, breads, yams and cranberry salad filled the refrigerator. Fortunately, Mrs. Anderson across the street let them keep the huge turkey in her extra refrigerator.

"Uncle Dwayne's family and Grandma and Grandpa get in on Wednesday afternoon," Mrs. Pearson explained to Sam. " I'll get off work at noon, which gives me time to pick them up at the airport, get back here, fix dinner, eat and make it to church."

But the day before Thanksgiving, they awoke to a world of snow. "Sam," her mom called from the kitchen, "could you please turn on the news so we can get the weather report?"

When Sam turned on the TV, she gasped. "Mom! They're having a blizzard in Michigan! The airports are all snowed in!"

Her dad rushed in, still holding his shaver. After watching a minute, he said, "This doesn't look good at all, Jean."

"It's still early," Mrs. Pearson protested. "Maybe the runways will get clear in time for them to still get out."

But they didn't. Sam's family's flight was delayed hour after hour, then finally canceled altogether. Grandma Pearson called from the airport. "We'll try again Thursday," she said. "We could still get there in time for Thanksgiving dinner." So Sam's family went alone to the Thanksgiving Eve service.

The next morning, Thanksgiving Day, the blizzard in Michigan was even worse. When Grandma Pearson called this time, she was crying. "I'm sorry, Sam, darling," she said, "but we'll get together at Christmas, for sure."

Mrs. Pearson looked around the kitchen. Then she started to cry, too. "Look at this food! Enough for an army! We'll never be able to eat it all. Not even with Todd's family coming over.

What a shame for it to go to waste!"

Sam was disappointed, too. She stared at the pies, yams, baked beans, cranberry salad, bowls of popcorn and nuts, candy corn, pickles and dinner rolls. Even her homemade pumpkin bread.

"Yuck!" she muttered. She grabbed a nut and the nutcracker and crunched it as hard as she could. "This is the nuttiest Thanksgiving of my entire life. Thanksgiving's no fun without lots of people around."

That's when she remembered where Miss Kotter would be spending the holiday. Jumping up, she said, "I have an idea!" Then she told her parents about the Thanksgiving Day meal at the Circleville Rescue Mission and suggested that they take all of their food there to help Miss Kotter.

"That's a great idea, Sam," her dad said. "But Todd's family is due here any minute. We'll have to see what they think about it first."

"Sounds great," said Sam's Uncle Todd when they arrived a few minutes later. "And when we get back, we can play in the snow. Snowmen, snow forts, snow angels, sledding. What do you say, Suzie?"

Suzie made a sour face. But everyone convinced her that playing with the other kids at the shelter might be fun. So they packed the vans and they were all on their way.

As Sam's family carried pots, plates and platters into the mission, people waiting in line outside smiled and cheered. There were piles of snow everywhere, but Sam noticed some of those in line didn't have warm coats to wear.

Inside, row after row of tables and benches had been set up, all ready for the feast. Miss Kotter helped everyone wash their hands and put on aprons, caps and plastic gloves. She had her hair pulled back off her neck so she wouldn't get stray hair in the food. Sam laughed. "Miss Kotter, you really are a PT today!"

Sam's dad and Uncle Todd went to work carving the turkeys. Even Sam's pumpkin bread was brought out to share. When all the food was ready to serve, the hungry guests were invited in. The shelter director led in prayer. Then the kitchen crew began serving.

As the children finished eating, they were invited into a playroom. Sam started a video for them and got out some games and puzzles. Petie and Suzie played "house" with the younger ones while Sam showed the older ones how to crack nuts and make toys out of the empty shells.

When the volunteers finally got a chance to eat, Miss Kotter sat across from Sam. "Well, Sam," she asked, "what do you think of all this?"

Sam thought a minute. "I miss my Grandma and Grandpa and the rest of our family. At first I thought this was the 'nuttiest Thanksgiving' of my life. But now, Miss Kotter, I think it's the very best one."

· Good News · from God's Word

Maybe you think kings and queens are so rich that they never have to be thankful for anything. But here's a Bible story about a great queen who helped all her people to be thankful to God.

A Queen's Thankfulness

from Esther 2-10

Esther wanted to help others. Because she was true to God, she and all of God's people had reason to give thanks.

"Hail, the great Queen Esther!" That's how people throughout the Persian Empire addressed this beautiful woman. Only a few knew that she was a Jew, one of God's people. One who did know was her cousin Mordecai, a very brave and kind man. Esther's husband, the great King Xerxes, was pleased with Mordecai for warning him that some people were planning to kill him. The king gave Mordecai great honor in the kingdom.

Esther was glad for her cousin. But one of the king's officials wasn't. Haman wanted all the glory and honor for himself. He knew Mordecai was a Jew. So he tricked the king into signing a law to kill all the Jews. That way, Haman thought, he could be rid of pesky Mordecai. But Haman didn't know that Esther was a Jew, too!

Brave Esther stood up for her people. Not only was evil Haman punished, but eventually all of Esther's people had peace and prosperity. The king promoted Mordecai to second in command over the entire empire. Only the king himself had more power. But, unlike Haman, Mordecai used all his power for good.

To celebrate, God's people held a great feast of thanksgiving. All over the empire they cooked and partied and gave each other presents. Everyone helped the poor, too. This time of joy, called Purim, is still celebrated every spring by Jews all over the world.

A Verse to Remember

Thanks be to God!

— 1 Corinthians 15:57

Got a Gratitude Attitude?

Write below some things in your life for which you should be thankful: family, home, friends, clothing, etc. After each item, write the name of whom you should thank for that blessing. (Maybe you need to thank several people.) Then go ahead and thank them. Jot down the date when you do it.

I am thankful for: ______________________________

I should thank: __________________

I did it! _________

I am thankful for:_______________________________

I should thank:__________________

I did it! _________

Going Nuts!

Fall is a great time for gathering and using nuts. Not only are they highly nutritious, they are crunchy and tasty as well. And so much fun to open with nutcrackers! You can add them to fudge, cookies, cakes, coffee cakes, salads and waffles. Or sprinkle some over ice cream. Thank God for these natural food gifts. Share them with others.

If you buy whole nuts still in their shells, such as English walnuts, you can use them in a game as "nutballs" to shoot through an embroidery hoop into a wastebasket. Here are some fun ideas for empty walnut shells:

- Glue or paint faces on them for finger puppets.
- Turn them upside-down, fill them with clay and push tiny artificial flowers in the clay to make a miniature flower pot.
- In a shallow pan of water, have a "boat race" of shellboats. Attach toothpicks and paper sails to the shellboats with clay, glue or chewing gum.

- Fill the bottom half of a shell with old beads or tiny wads of gold or silver foil. Cover this shell with the top shell to make a treasure chest.
- Play the shell game with shell halves and dry peas or beans. Place a bean under a shell when a friend is not looking, then ask, "Which shell is the bean under?"
- Fold up a note that says "You win!" and place it inside two nut halves. Tape them together. Put the empty nut in a bowl full of uncracked nuts. Have your friends select nuts and crack them until they find the note. Give the winner some of that good food you made from nuts!

continued on next page...

- Write a happy note to each person with whom you share Thanksgiving dinner that says you are glad he or she came to dinner. Fold it and put it inside the shell halves from one nut and tie the halves together with pretty ribbon.

Secret Letter

Add a "T" for "thankful" in space 5 of your Secret Birthday Circle on page 44.

Chapter 15

It's a Mall World, After All

The Saturday after Thanksgiving, the PTs got together at Sara's house. Outside, the world was still a winter wonderland. Inside, they sipped hot spiced cider, listened to CDs and munched on popcorn.

After their snack, Sara waved her arms. "All right, everybody, business time. I called everyone over here for one reason. All together now: what do we need to plan for?"

"Miss Kotter's birthday!" the others shouted in unison.

"Right. All fall we've been talking about giving her a present and a party. But what kind of present? What kind of party? And how are we going to pay for it all?"

Sam dumped out her change purse. "Okay, let's see what we've got."

After everyone emptied their pockets, Sara counted the pile of money. "$23.39! What can we do with that?"

Maria thought a minute. "Well, we can save money by doing our own food for the party. You know, snacks like we're eating right now. Salad, maybe lasagna. We can get the frozen kind and bake it. Cake, too, of course. And something to drink."

Sara nodded. "I could ask Mom if she can drive us over to Midway Mall. Maybe we'll get some more ideas there."

"If we can get through the crowds," added LaToya. "Remember, Christmas shopping's started!"

Sara's mom agreed to drive them and help them select a gift. As LaToya predicted, the mall was a madhouse! Parking was very hard to find. But once inside, the girls oohed and aahed at all the sparkling decorations. Trees, garland, lights and glitter were everywhere. "Just think, all of this is because Jesus came to earth!" Le said.

"But so many of these people rushing around here are only thinking of what they'll buy or what they'll sell or what they'll get," replied Sam. "It's too bad they don't remember why God sent Jesus here — to be our Savior."

The girls zipped in and out of department stores, gift shops, shoe stores, music and video stores and stores of every description. After an hour or more of flying all over the mall, LaToya complained, "My feet hurt! I gotta sit on this bench for a minute or I'm going to drop."

The bench was right in front of Max's Arts & Crafts. Mrs. Fields looked in its window. Then she smiled. "Yes, go ahead and rest, girls. I just had a great idea. Sara, could you come with me?" Then they rushed into the store.

Le rubbed her aching feet. After a while she sighed, "We might as well go back home. This is never going to work."

Just then mother and daughter returned, both beaming. "Yes, it is going to work, Le," Sara said. "But you're going to have to trust us."

The other girls looked at each other. "Trust you?" they asked with uncertainty.

"Yes. Give Mom and me the money for Miss Kotter. We promise to come up with a great present — maybe even four of them! But you've got to trust us. It'll have to be a secret until we have everything ready. We'll wrap, do the cards — the whole thing. The rest of you can take care of the food. OK?"

Sam stared at her. Give up their money? Just

like that? "Well, OK," Sam said after a long pause. "We'll trust you to do your part, and you trust us to do ours."

But she was still feeling funny about it the next morning in Sunday school. Their Bible lesson was about Mary being told that she would be the mother of God's Son, Jesus, and how she trusted God and believed His Word. "Trusting someone to do something they promise is hard sometimes, isn't it?" Sam asked her teacher.

"Yes," Miss Kotter answered. "The secret is knowing and trusting the person who makes that promise. Even though this was a new promise to Mary, she already knew God, so she knew she could trust whatever He said to her."

Then Miss Kotter told them that "T" for "trusting" was the last secret letter on the Secret Birthday Circle. "Now everyone start up here at space 1 and go around the circle. What does it say?"

"TURN TO THE LORD," they said.

"That's cool, Miss Kotter!" Sam exclaimed. "But what are the four spaces at the bottom for?'

Their teacher's eyes twinkled. "For me to know and you to find out — next week!"

That evening, all the youth groups met together with Pastor Andy as the speaker. "What would happen," he asked, "if someone showed up every day after school in uniform for football practice and went to all the games but never played in a real game because he never got around to joining the team?

"Some of you do that in your own lives. You

come to church every Sunday and join in the activities. That's great! But do you ever stop and ask yourself why?

"You know all about how to 'do' church," he continued. "Praise the Lord! But do you know God?

"You know all about the Gospel and Christianity. Hallelujah! But have you experienced Christ in your own life? Do you know Him as your personal Savior and friend?"

Afterward, Faith Church held its annual Christmas Advent prayer night. Sara slipped into the pew beside Sam. The quiet music and soft candles touched Sam's heart. "I'm sorry I didn't trust you right away this afternoon," she whispered. Sara squeezed her hand.

Then Sam thought about what Pastor Andy said. She knew what it meant to trust her friend Sara. But what did "trusting Jesus" really mean?

Soon it was time for the offering. As Sam reached into her wallet, she pulled out some change, including a quarter. She looked at the picture of George Washington and read the words: "In God We Trust." There was that "t" word again!

Dear God, she prayed silently. *I'm so confused. Please help me to know how to really trust You!*

To be continued in Chapter 16

· Good News · from God's Word

At first, Sam found it hard to trust Sara, even for something relatively small. This Bible story is about a young woman who had to trust God about something very, very big.

Mary's Trust in God's Word

FROM LUKE 1:26-38

Mary was so busy! She was very much in love with a young man named Joseph, an honest, hardworking carpenter. In fact, they were engaged to be married. Joseph was a fine young man who loved God as much as she did.

Then one day something wonderful happened. We don't know if Mary was sewing or praying or scrubbing the floor. Or even baking some delicious bread. But suddenly an angel was right beside her. Was she surprised! She was so frightened she almost couldn't breathe!

"Please don't be afraid," the angel said. "God is with you. He is going to give you a little baby boy. You will name Him 'Jesus.' He will be the Savior of His people, and His Kingdom will never end."

Mary knew from God's Word that the Messiah would come one day. In fact, she and Joseph had been praying for the Messiah to come very soon. She also hoped to have children one day after she and Joseph were married. But how could she have a baby before then?

"It will be a miracle," the angel explained, "through the power of God's Holy Spirit." Then he told her that her relative Elizabeth, an old woman, was going to have a special baby, too. "Nothing is impossible with God," the angel said.

"I trust God to do what is best," Mary said. "Whatever God wants for me is what I want, too."

A Verse to Remember

Trust in the name of the Lord.

— Zephaniah 3:12

Measuring Up

We turn to God in times of trouble. We pray for His help to pass a math test or make a home run or heal a sick friend. We look to Him for comfort, love and protection. We look to God for advice and direction in our lives. We study His Word to learn right from wrong.

However, turning to God means even more than that. It also means realizing that God is always loving, kind, pure, holy, righteous and helpful — never greedy, jealous, mean, gossipy or hateful. He always does what He promises to do. He always does what's right.

We don't. That's what "sin" means: not measuring up to God's standards. Turning to God means we realize we've done wrong and we know we need God's power to help us do what's right. It means believing that God sent His Son to die for us and be our Savior so that we can be His children forever.

Read the list on the next page. Circle how often you do each one.

Never	Sometimes	A Lot	Always

1. Fight with my brothers or sisters.

0	2	3	4

2. Talk back to my parents.

0	2	3	4

3. Goof off during class.

0	2	3	4

4. Say something mean about someone.

0 2 3 4

5. Let my mind wander during prayer.

0 2 3 4

6. Blow up in anger.

0 2 3 4

7. Snub or ignore someone.

0 2 3 4

8. Try to cheat or to shoplift.

0 2 3 4

9. Be jealous of someone.

0 2 3 4

10. Make fun of someone.

0 2 3 4

Now add up all your numbers.

What's your score? TOTAL ______

Anything over zero counts as sin. How do you measure up? See page 203 for Jesus' score.

In God We Trust

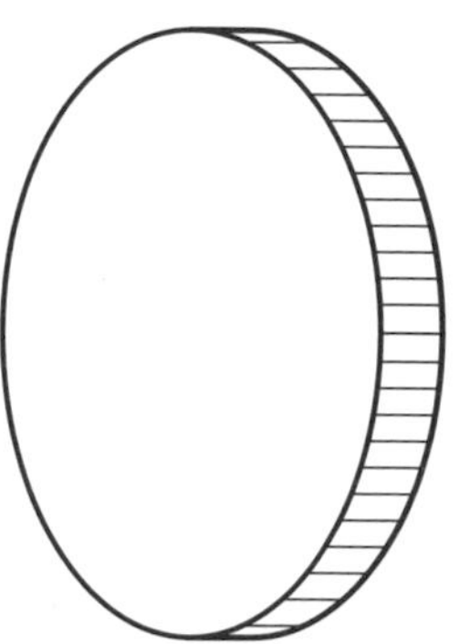

The U.S. quarter has the words "In God We Trust" on it, as Sam noticed. Print those words on this coin shape at right. Then, like Sam, think about what the words mean. You can't buy much with a quarter, but its message is priceless.

Secret Letter

Be sure to add a "T" for "trusting" in space 7 of your Secret Birthday Circle on page 44! This completes the circle. As Miss Kotter instructed, start with space 1 at the top right of the circle to read it. Copy the words in the spaces below. Remember, there will still be four blank spaces at the bottom of the circle.

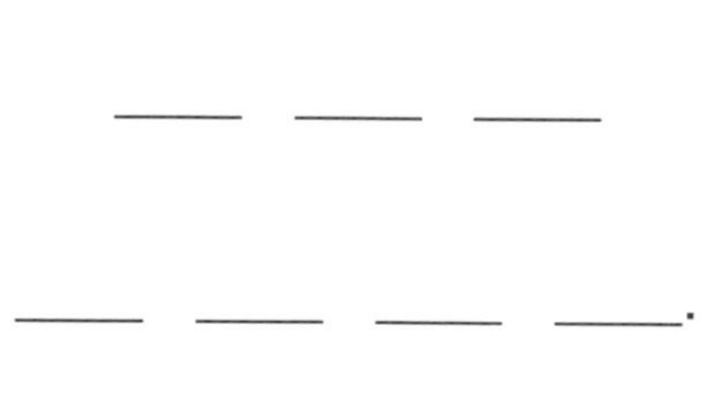

Chapter 16

4M2U or 4J2U?

The next Sunday morning, the sky was as clear and blue as Lucky Lake.

"Everything's going to be just perfect for this afternoon!" LaToya said excitedly when she saw Sam at church. "Mom said we could have Miss Kotter's party at my house. Le and I are making lasagna. Mom's doing the salad. Maria's bringing paper plates and cups. You're getting the cake. We've already got plenty of punch to drink and snacks. As long as Sara and her mom come through with the presents, we're set!"

"Oh, they will," Sam insisted. "Sara said they'd finish it up after church this morning."

That morning the class prayed for Maria's little sister, Lolita. She'd been coughing hard all night, so Mrs. Moreno kept her home from church. The class's Bible lesson was about Priscilla and her husband, Aquila. They were not only skilled tentmakers, but kind, loving people. When they saw that young Apollos wanted to love God, but that he didn't really understand about Jesus, they took time to tell Him the Good News about God's Son.

"Miss Kotter," Sam said, "what's the best way to learn about Jesus?"

The teacher smiled. "In Sunday school, in church services, in your youth group, reading your Bible or talking to others who love Jesus. But the best way of all is just to believe in Him as your Savior. Turn to God in faith to forgive you and cleanse you from sin. God will make you a new person through His Holy Spirit and you will be with God forever. That's what this week's Bible verse is all about."

Then the class read together: "Believe in the Lord Jesus, and you will be saved" from Acts 16:31. Miss Kotter continued, "Don't think of your life as something 4M2U — for me to use. Think of it as something 4J2U — for Jesus to use. Your body is to be a holy temple for His service." Then she told them that the four spaces at the bottom of the Secret Birthday Circle were for 4J2U.

"See you this afternoon," the PTs called to each other after church.

Just before party time, however, things suddenly fell apart. Maria's little sister got worse, with a high fever. "Your papa and I need to take her to the clinic," Mrs. Moreno told Maria. "You'll have to babysit your brothers while I'm gone."

Maria jumped up. "Mama, no! Miss Kotter's party's this afternoon! What if you're not back in time?"

"Well, call LaToya's mom and see if it's OK to take the boys over there with you. Or invite everyone to have the party over here at our house. I'm sorry, Maria, but your sister's health comes first." Then they were gone.

"Of course Juan and Ricardo can come over," Mrs. Thomas said. "Granny B. will be delighted to have them." By the time Maria and her twin brothers arrived, Sam was showing up with the cake — and Petie.

"I'm sorry," Sam sighed. "Dad had to work today, so Mom's taking him dinner at the station where he works. Which means I have to watch Petie. Kind of a downer."

Granny B. laughed. "Land sakes, not a downer — downright delightful! Come on, Petie, I'll race you to my room. The other boys are playing in there. Wait 'til you see my hamsters."

As Granny B. and Petie headed off down the hall, the doorbell rang. Sara, her mom, Mrs. Tran and Miss Kotter all arrived at the same time. "Too bad!" Sam whispered to Maria. "Now we won't know what Miss Kotter's presents are until she opens them!"

What fun everyone had! There was plenty of

lasagna and salad. The cake was Mrs. Pearson's chocolate with lots of nuts. "Suzie and me cracked the nuts," Petie bragged. And to top it off, rocky road ice cream! For entertainment, Le and LaToya and Mrs. Tran all played while everyone sang "Happy Birthday." Then Granny B. sang "Anchors Aweigh" in honor of Miss Kotter's boyfriend, Bob, who was in the Navy.

Afterward, Sara and Le brought in two pieces of luggage on wheels, tied up with big red ribbons. Sam was puzzled. Sara didn't have enough money for that!

"Miss Kotter," Sara began, "we know the homeless women at the rescue mission usually don't have anything to carry their things in. So Le's mom is donating these bags for the mission. Your gifts are in Bag 2. But you have to open Bag 1 first."

Bag 1 was filled with gifts for the rescue mission. Homemade aprons and baby clothes from Granny B., and towels, wash cloths and hand soap from Mrs. Thomas. Sam's mom donated toothbrushes, toothpaste, lipstick, baby powder and diapers. Mrs. Moreno had given her children's outgrown clothes, all cleaned and pressed. Mrs. Fields had organized all of this without any of the girls knowing, except Sara.

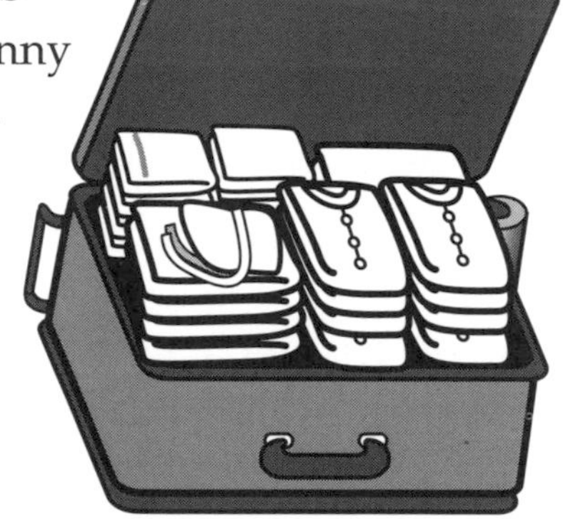

By the time Miss Kotter opened Bag 2, Sam

was almost too excited to sit still. For gift wrap, Sara and her mom used scraps of beautiful, unused wallpaper. They even made their own ribbon by braiding strands of yarn.

Even more wonderful were the gifts. First, there was a deep red, floral quilted cover for Miss Kotter's Bible. Sara and her mom had sewn it themselves, complete with zippers and pockets. one of which held a beautiful gold pen. From the same fabric, they had made a matching picture frame ("for Bob's picture," they said) and a pin cushion.

Then Sara pulled out a matching little drawstring bag lined with gold satin. "This is the most special gift of all," she told Miss Kotter. "We hope you like it."

When Miss Kotter opened the bag, out fell a necklace, bracelet and pair of earrings. "Oooh!" she cooed.

"Oooh!" cried the other girls, too.

"Oh, Sara, we're so glad your mom is an artist!"

"These are cool!"

"It's a Secret Birthday Circle to wear, Miss Kotter," Sara explained. The whole jewelry set had been made of gold twine and small, square letter beads. There were tiny knots in between them. The necklace read "TURN TO THE LORD." Each earring had two beads: one read, "4J," and the other, "2U." So together they read, "4J2U."

"That's why we couldn't do the earrings until today," Sara explained. "Because we didn't know what those last four spaces would be!"

The bracelet said: "LSSLMK."

Miss Kotter smiled, but looked puzzled. "Is this English?"

"That's for all our names," Sara said. "LaToya, Sam, Sara, Le, Maria — and you, too, Miss Kotter."

Just then, Mrs. Moreno called. The doctor had given them medicine for Lolita, and she was going to be fine.

"Yeah!" Maria cheered.

Miss Kotter had tears in her eyes. "Thank you, girls. I think this has been the best birthday of my life. Thank you so much for the gifts for me and for the rescue mission."

Mrs. Tran smiled. "We're glad you liked them, Miss Kotter. And thank you for being Le's teacher. I have enjoyed attending your church's services, too."

Later, while everyone else was talking, Mrs. Tran quietly said to Miss Kotter, "I'm sorry, but I have a question to ask you. An important question. I have been going to your church and listening to all this talk about Jesus and about God. How do you know your God is real?"

To be continued in Chapter 17

· Good News · from God's Word

If someone wanted you to tell him or her about Jesus, what would you say? Here's a Bible story about a couple who loved to tell people about their best friend, Jesus.

Priscilla Explains the Gospel

FROM ACTS 18:1-4, 18-26

After Paul became a Christian, he traveled around telling people about Jesus. One place he visited was Corinth, Greece. There he met Priscilla and her husband, Aquila. They were tentmakers with lots of work. Since Paul knew how to make tents, he stayed and helped them, and they helped him tell people about Jesus.

Later, God called Paul to Syria. Aquila and Priscilla decided to go with him. They settled in Ephesus, in the land we now call Turkey. Paul went other places after that, but his tentmaking friends stayed there and helped the new Christians.

One day Priscilla and Aquila met an enthusiastic young Egyptian named Apollos. He told everyone He met about God. Apollos loved God and knew His Word. He also knew God would send His Son — but he didn't know that Jesus had already come!

Priscilla and her husband could have embarrassed him in front of everyone. Instead, they invited him to their home. There they told him the wonderful news: Jesus had been born, died on a cross and then rose again from the dead. Apollos was so excited! He traveled to many other cities and led people to Christ.

A Verse to Remember

Believe in the Lord Jesus,
and you will be saved.

— Acts 16:31

What About You?

Paul wrote, "For to me, to live is Christ" (Philippians 1:21). That's another way of saying, "I give my life for Jesus to use." God wants us to put Him first, but it is easy to sin and put other things before Him. Here are a few things some people want to be the most important in their lives:

food	clothes	money	career
fame	family	status	romance
sports	fine house	new car	education
beauty	power	fun	popularity

Is there anything that you are putting before God in your life? If so, write it here:

________________________.

Take a minute right now to ask God to help you put Him first in your life instead of whatever else comes your way. Nothing should be more important to us than Him!

"Beady" Eyes Are Nice!

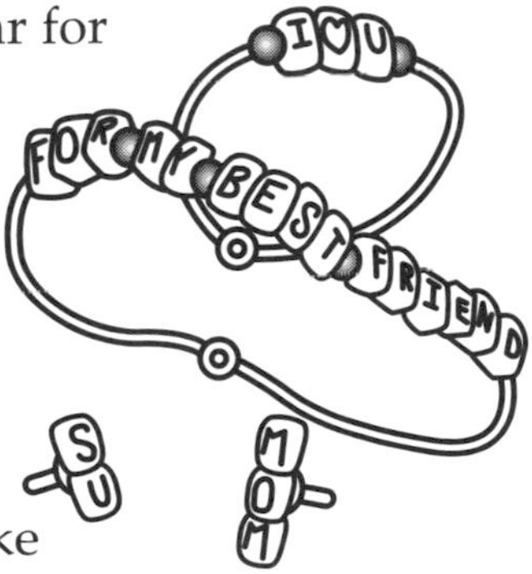

Beads have been popular for jewelry-making for thousands of years. They can be made of metal, glass, plastic, ceramic, shell or polished stones or gems. Or they might be made from nature, such as seeds or oyster pearls. You can also make your own beads from clay, paper or fabric. To learn how, ask someone who does a lot of crafts. Or go to the library and find a how-to book on jewelry.

You can find beads in craft stores, including the letter beads that Sara and Mrs. Fields used. For an eye-catching look, select bright-colored or metallic twine. Or even try the elastic kind. Then start adding beads from the center outward. You can make small knots between the beads. You might also add colored beads in between the letter ones. Your bracelet may spell out someone's name (even your own) or "to my best friend" or even "4J2U" like Sara and her mom wrote on Miss Kotter's earrings. Whatever you do, be creative and honor God with your work.

Secret Letters

Write "4J2U" in the four blanks at the bottom of the Secret Birthday Circle on page 44. To help you remember what "4J2U" means, write the words in the spaces below:

_____ _____ _____

_____ _____ _____ _____ _____

_____ _____

_____ _____ _____

Chapter 17

Best Birthday Present of All

Sam was so shocked, she wasn't even sure she was breathing. One minute the girls and some of their mothers were having a great time at Miss Kotter's birthday party. The next, Le's mom, a shy, quiet Buddhist who had started attending Faith Church, suddenly became very intense and serious.

"Miss Kotter," Mrs. Tran repeated, "how do

you know your God is real?"

Then she added, "You see, Buddhism teaches that there are many gods. What's important in Buddhism is being a good person like Buddha. That means doing a lot of good deeds and thinking many good thoughts. Then maybe you'll be a better person the next time you're born. This goes on and on through many lives. Finally, if you are very good or very lucky, you might become perfect." Then she sighed. "But being perfect is so very hard to do."

Miss Kotter hugged her. "It's not just hard, it's impossible! Only the God who created our whole universe is perfect." Then she told Mrs. Tran the Bible story of Lydia and how Lydia was thrilled to learn that she didn't have to be perfect. God had sent His perfect Son to die for Lydia and for everyone else, Miss Kotter explained. All she had to do was believe in Jesus as her Savior. That's why the Gospel is called "Good News." God does everything for us. We only have to believe it.

"So how do I know God is real?" Miss Kotter continued. "How do I know Jesus helps me every day? I know it right here," she said as she pointed to a Bible in the Thomases' living room, "here" as she pointed to the girls around her, "and here" as she pointed to her heart.

Mrs. Tran was quiet a moment. "That's what Le's dad kept telling me. But at the time, all my friends were Buddhist. I was afraid not to think like them. But since moving here to Circleville, I have met so many Christians — like you, and these girls, and the people at your church. You have so much joy, so much peace, just as my husband did. My god doesn't give me that. Only your God seems to give it."

After Miss Kotter and the other women prayed with Mrs. Tran, Le burst into tears. "Oh, Mom! I've been praying for you for so long! Now we're not just a family, we're a Christian family!"

Then everyone sang "Happy Birthday" again, but this time to Le's mom because she had just been "born again" as God's child. "This is the best birthday present of all for me!" cried Miss Kotter.

Sam and Petie could hardly wait to share the good news with their own mother. "It was so cool, Mom!" Sam exclaimed when they reached home. "How old were you when you became a Christian, Mom?"

"About your age, Sam."

"Wow!" Petie piped up. "When did you become one, Sam?"

"Me?" Sam stared at him. "Are you crazy? We've been going to church all our lives. Obviously we were born Christians. Speaking of which, I've got to get ready for Zone 56." And she rushed off to her room.

At the meeting, Le bubbled over with news about her mom's decision. "I'm so thankful I made my own decision for Christ last year," she told everyone. "My mom's been so unhappy for so long. I'm her only living relative, you know. But tonight she's so happy!"

"But, Le!" Sam remarked. "You weren't born in Vietnam like your mother. You were born right here in the U.S. like me. So you couldn't have become a Christian last year. You were already one!"

"Sam," Pastor Andy said, "Jesus was born in a stable. But that didn't make Him a horse, did it?" Then he explained that it's not where we live or the color of our skin that makes us God's child. Everyone is a child of God because He created each of us in His own image. But it is when we decide to believe in His Word, just as Lydia did, that we become Christians who can live with Him forever. Each person has to make that decision for him or herself.

Sam thought about what Pastor Andy said. She thought about it all the way home. She thought about it as she did her homework, brushed her teeth and ironed her shirt for school the next day. After she put on her pajamas, Sam grabbed her Bible off of her desk. Sitting on the edge of her bed, she read again the story of Lydia from her Bible.

Then she prayed, "Dear God, thank You for loving me. Please forgive me for all I've done wrong. I do believe that your Son Jesus died for my sins and then rose again. Fill my heart and life. Help me to serve Jesus every single day. In Jesus' name. Amen."

Wow! She did it! She really, really did it! And God was really right there in her heart!

Sam snuggled down under her comforter. Tomorrow would be a new day. The first of a whole new life as Sam Pearson, God's child!

· Good News · from God's Word

When we have good news to tell, we want everyone to know. That's why Paul and his friends wanted to travel all over the world. They had Good News to tell about Jesus. In fact, the very best news in the world!

Lydia's Decision for Christ

FROM ACTS 16:11-15

Paul and his friends had something they wanted to share with everyone they could: the Good News about Jesus! They traveled several hundred miles, going from city to city. Then one day God called them to sail away to Greece.

The first city they came to was called Philippi. There were no Christians there yet. But there were probably a few Jews in that city who loved God.

On the Sabbath, Paul went down to the river to see if any of the Jews were meeting there to pray. He didn't see any men, but he did find some women praying. One of them was a businesswoman named Lydia. Lydia sold beautiful purple fabric. She was a kind woman who hungered to know more about God. She knew that the Greek gods could bring no peace or joy.

Paul and his friends told her about Jesus. She was so thrilled, she made her decision for Christ right then and there. So did the rest of her family! Everyone was baptized.

When Lydia found out that Paul didn't have a place to stay in Philippi, she invited him and his friends to be her guests. Paul gained a friend in Lydia, but she gained an even better friend: Jesus.

A Verse to Remember

Trust in the Lord with all your heart.

— Proverbs 3:5

What About You?

Which of the following statements are true about you? Check "yes" or "no."

1. I have definitely asked Jesus into my heart, to be my Savior and Lord.

   Yes ___ No ___

   If I have, this is when I did it:

   ____

2. I know that I am God's child.

   Yes ___ No ___

3. I know God sent His Son, Jesus, to die for my sins.

   Yes ___ No ___

4. God's Holy Spirit lives in my heart to guide me every day.

   Yes ___ No ___

5. I pray and talk to God, my heavenly Father.

   Yes ___ No ___

6. I read God's Word, the Bible:

   Every day ___ Every week ___

   When I think of it ___ Never ___

Do You Have Two Birthdays?

Being "born again" means becoming a new person through faith in Christ. You may look the same on the outside. You may even act the same, at first. But as you ask God daily to help you, and try to live for Him, you will become more and more like Jesus. What a wonderful way to be! You'll even spend eternity with Him in heaven!

If you've already made that decision, praise the Lord! Aren't you glad? But if you haven't yet, this is a great time to do so. Don't think that you need to wait until you are older. You are at a perfect age to become a Christian. That way you'll have Jesus with you every single day, right on through middle school, high school and beyond! Here's what to do if you're ready to make such a decision right now:

Get away to a quiet place where you will not be disturbed. Tell God you're sorry for all your sins. You can say it out loud or to yourself. God "hears" you either way. Thank Him for loving you so much that He gave His Son, Jesus, to die for you. Believe in Jesus as your Savior from sin. Ask Him to come into your heart and life and make you all new. Then praise Him for doing so!

If you just prayed that prayer now, sign and date the certificate on the next page. Write that same information inside your Bible.

Now tell someone, like your parents, pastor or Sunday school teacher, the Good News about what just happened to you!

I made my decision
for Christ today
signed:

Extra Stuff!

The following pages contain bonus Ponytail Girls activities especially for you. In this section you will find ways to make your prayer life better and a few pages to jot down your thoughts about the PTs, your life, your dreams or whatever you want! You will also find information on forming your own Ponytail Girls Club, including membership cards.

At the end of this section, check out the coupon for a **free scrunchie!**

My Prayer Partners

It is very comforting and helpful to have someone else praying along with you. The person may be close to you — even right beside you! Or your prayer partner might be far away. But you know your partner is praying for the very same things for which you are praying. You are praying for that person's needs, too.

You may have one prayer partner, such as your best friend. Or you could have many, such as your Sunday school teacher, grandmother, pen pal and sister. Write below the name or names of each prayer partner you have. If you do not have a prayer partner, ask someone to partner with you. Beside each name write what that person would like you to pray for. When a prayer has been answered, put a big check mark beside it. Also write the date and "PTL" (for "praise the Lord"!).

My Prayer Partners	Prayer Requests	Answer
______________________	______________________	❑
______________________	______________________	❑
______________________	______________________	❑
______________________	______________________	❑
______________________	______________________	❑
______________________	______________________	❑

My Prayer Partners	Prayer Requests	Answer
________	________	❑
________	________	❑
________	________	❑
________	________	❑
________	________	❑
________	________	❑
________	________	❑
________	________	❑
________	________	❑
________	________	❑
________	________	❑
________	________	❑
________	________	❑
________	________	❑
________	________	❑
________	________	❑
________	________	❑

This is a handy place for you to write down what you want to pray about. Of course, God wants you to ask Him for help with your problems. But don't forget to thank Him for His loving care, His glorious creation, His Son Jesus and all the other blessings He gives you.

Date	Prayer Request	Answer

Date	Prayer Request	Answer

My Sweet Dreams Diary

Z Z Z Z

Every girl has dreams for the future. You also probably enjoy thinking about things that happened a long time ago, and what is happening to you right now. That's what a diary is for. In it, you can write each day's thoughts or special events you don't want to forget. You may like writing in it every day, or just once in a while.

We have included a few pages for you to start a Sweet Dreams Diary. It starts below and continues on the next page. On the date line, include the month, day and year to help you remember what happened and when. Then just write whatever you want!

When you use up the space on these pages, you'll probably want to continue writing. Use a binder, tablet or diary to hold more of your "sweet dreams." Write your name, the title "My Sweet Dreams Diary" and your beginning date on the cover. Sweet dreams!

sweet dreams • sweet dreams • sweet dreams • sweet dreams • sweet dreams

Date ____________

____

____

____

____

____

Date ____________

Date ____________

Date ____________

sweet dreams • sweet dreams • sweet dreams • sweet dreams • sweet dreams • sweet dreams • sweet dreams

The Ponytail Girls Club

Would you like to be a part of a Ponytail Girls Club? You can be a PT yourself, of course. But it's much more fun if one of your friends joins with you. Or even five or six of them! There is no cost. You can read the Ponytail Girls stories together, do the puzzles and other activities, study the Bible stories, and learn the Bible verses.

If your friends buy their own Ponytail Girls books, you can all write in yours at the same time. Arrange a regular meeting time and place, and plan to do special things together, just like the PTs do in the stories, such as shopping, Bible study, homework, or helping others.

Have each girl in your Ponytail Girls club fill out the survey on pages 195 and 196. Then trace or copy the membership cards on page 193 and give one to each PT in your group.

Membership Cards

Trace or photocopy these cards. Fill them out, color them in and give one to each member of your Ponytail Girls club. Be sure to put your membership card in your wallet or another special place for safekeeping!

____

is a member in good standing of
The Ponytail Girls Club.

____
Signature

____
Date

____

is a member in good standing of
The Ponytail Girls Club.

____
Signature

____
Date

My name is ____________________________.

I am in grade __________.

I am _____ years old.

My hair color is ________________________.

My hair is (check one) short __ long __ in between __ .

My best friend is ________________________.

When I grow up, I want to be a _____________.

My mother's name is _____________________.

My father's name is ______________________.

continued on next page…

My sisters' names are ______________________________.

My brothers' names are ____________________________.

My favorite teacher is ______________________________.

My favorite color is ________________________________.

My favorite food is _________________________________.

My favorite type of music is _______________________.

My favorite style of shoes is _______________________.

My favorite sport is ________________________________.

My best talent is __________________________________.

My worst fault is __________________________________.

My favorite Bible story is __________________________.

Bible Verses to Remember and Share

These are the Bible verses the PTs studied throughout this book. Write them on pretty paper and learn them. Share your favorite with someone else!

God is our refuge and strength,
an ever-present help in trouble.
~ Psalm 46:1

My help comes from the Lord.
~ Psalm 121:2

Trust in the Lord with all your heart.
~ Proverbs 3:5

A friend loves at all times.
~ Proverbs 17:17

Obey the Lord your God.
~ Jeremiah 26:13

Trust in the name of the Lord.
~ Zephaniah 3:12

What I have I give you.
~ Acts 3:6

Believe in the Lord Jesus, and you will be saved.
~ Acts 16:31

Thanks be to God!
~ 1 Corinthians 15:57

continued on next page…

We work with you for your joy.
~ 2 Corinthians 1:24

God loves a cheerful giver.
~ 2 Corinthians 9:7

Serve one another in love.
~ Galatians 5:13

Look not only to your own interests,
but also to the interests of others.
~ Philippians 2:4

In everything, by prayer and petition, with thanksgiving,
present your requests to God.
~ Philippians 4:6

Whatever you do, work at it with all your heart,
as working for the Lord.
~ Colossians 3:23

Show this same diligence to the very end.
~ Hebrews 6:11

Do not forget to entertain strangers.
~ Hebrews 13:2

Glossary (glos/ə rē)

Aquila: *uh-kwill-uh*

Buenos dias: *good morning*

Caitlin: *kate-lin*

Canaan: *kay-nun*

Compost: *kahm-post*

Dorcas: *door-kus*

Eli: *ee-lie*

Elisha: *ee-lie-sha*

Ephesus: *eh-fu-sus*

Euphrates: *you-fray-teez*

Haman: *hay-mun*

Haran: *har* (like "far")-*on*

Israel: *iz-ree-ul*

Jairus: *jayr-us*

Juan: *whan*

LaToya: *lah-toy-yuh*

Le: *lee*

Leprosy: *leh-pro-see*

Mordecai: *more-duh-ki*

Naaman: *nay-muhn*

Philippi: *fill-i-pie*

Piñata: *peen-yah-tuh*

Purim: *pure-ihm*

Shunem: *shoe-num*

Si: *yes*

Terah: *tair-uh*

Ur: rhymes with *"fur"*

Xerxes: *zurk-zeez*

Answers to Puzzles

Chapter 1

What About You?, p. 25

1. All the names

A Sinking Feeling Maze, p. 26

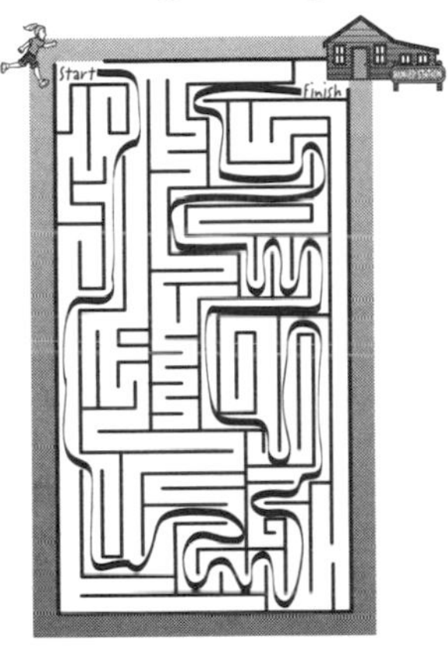

Chapter 2

What About You?, p. 33

SHE PRAYED TO GOD

A Prayer Is Quiz, p. 34

1. D
2. A
3. B
4. E
5. F
6. H
7. C
8. G

Chapter 3

What About You?, p. 43

3. No
4. All

Chapter 6

What About You?, p. 71

1. F
2. F
3. T
4. F
5. T
6. T
7. T
8. F

Chapter 7

When You Need Help, pp. 81-82

When you are stumped
On what to do,
Ask God for help.
He will see you through!

Chapter 8

4J2U, p. 93

Chapter 9

Friends or Frights? pp. 100-101

1. no, no
2. no, no
3. no, no

continued on next page…

4. yes, yes
5. yes, yes
6. no, no
7. no, no
8. yes, yes
9. no, no
10. yes, yes

How Sweet It Is!, pp. 101-102

2. D
4. E
6. C
8. B
10. A

Chapter 10

Happy Searching!, p. 111

D	O	D	I	S	H	E	S	E	T	T	A	B	L	E
U	X	X	M	D	E	E	W	X	X	G	C	X	X	X
S	R	D	O	P	L	X	E	E	S	I	L	S	X	X
T	A	L	O	O	P	X	E	D	C	V	E	W	C	W
M	C	I	R	L	W	K	P	G	R	E	A	O	L	O
O	H	U	N	I	I	N	X	E	U	M	N	D	E	N
W	S	B	A	S	T	I	S	Y	B	A	B	N	A	S
L	A	V	E	H	H	T	X	A	S	S	I	I	N	L
A	W	A	L	K	D	O	G	R	H	S	R	W	S	E
W	A	C	C	T	I	X	X	D	O	A	D	H	I	V
N	S	U	P	N	N	X	X	X	W	G	C	S	D	O
I	H	U	O	I	N	X	X	X	E	E	A	A	E	H
R	D	M	H	A	E	W	E	S	R	X	G	W	W	S
O	O	X	S	P	R	E	K	A	C	A	E	K	A	B
N	G	R	A	K	E	L	E	A	V	E	S	X	L	X
X	X	M	E	N	D	T	A	C	D	E	E	F	K	X

Chapter 11

To Be or Not to Be, p. 121

Chapter 12

What About You?, pp. 128-129

1. c
2. b
3. a

Doing Figure 8's, p. 129

Serve God eagerly
With love and grace,
A helping hand,
And a smiling face.

Chapter 15

Measuring Up, pp. 160-161

Jesus' score would be zero. He never did anything wrong.

Chapter 16

Here is the complete solution to the
Secret Birthday Circle:

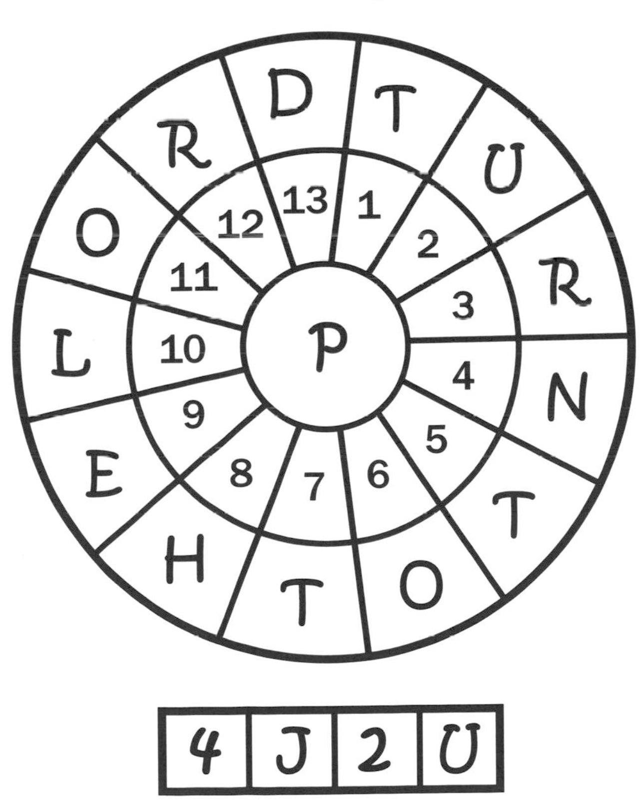

GET A FREE SCRUNCHIE!

The Ponytail Girls love to give each other gifts. Here is one for you: a free scrunchie! Just fill out the form below and enclose a check or money order for $2.20 to cover shipping and handling. Also, we would love to hear more about you and your thoughts, so please fill out the form on the other side, too.

____
My name

____
My address

____
City State Zip

____
Parent's signature

My birth date: ____/____/____
month/day/year

❑ Send me a scrunchie and a free catalog!
My $2.20 check or money order is enclosed.

❑ Send my friend a free catalog, too!

____
My friend's name

____
Address

____
City State Zip

Mail this form to: Ponytails • Legacy Press • P.O. Box 261129 • San Diego, CA 92196

Which of *The Ponytail Girls* books have you read?

- ❑ Meet the Ponytail Girls
- ❑ The Impossible Christmas Present
- ❑ Lost on Monster Mountain
- ❑ A Stormy Spring
- ❑ Escape from Camp Porcupine

My favorite PT is: ______________________.

I am in a Ponytail Girls Club. ❑ yes ❑ no

I am in another club. ❑ yes ❑ no

The name of my club is: ______________________.

My favorite thing to do is: ______________________________________.

My favorite book is: ______________________.

because: ____

My favorite magazine is: ______________________.

because: ____

Attention: Christian babysitters!

This is the only manual you will need to be the best babysitter on the block— and to share about God with others. *The Official Christian Babysitting Guide* is packed with everything you want to know about taking care of kids. Step-by-step instructions will help you learn the best ways to change a diaper, feed a baby or calm a scared child. Plus, get ideas for keeping kids busy with pages and pages of crafts, games, snacks and songs. Most importantly, you will find Scriptures and strategies for serving God as you serve families. Get *The Official Christian Babysitting Guide* and find out how you can be a blessing as you baby-sit!

LP 48021
ISBN 1-58411-027-9

You're not just a girl. You're one of God's Girls!

Hey, girls, get ready to add some sparkle to your look and a lot of fun to your life. *God's Girls* is packed with tips and ideas to help you make cool crafts. Plus you will read about Bible women and learn how to be a faithful Christian. There is even space included for you to write your deepest thoughts and dreams. So come on and join the party…you are one of *God's Girls!*

LP48011
ISBN 1-58411-020-1

LP48012
ISBN 1-58411-021-X